THE CHIEF SINNERS OBJECTS OF THE CHOICEST MERCY

STEPHEN CHARNOCK

MONERGISM BOOKS
WEST LINN, OR

Edited and modernized by Monergism Books.

Copyright © 2023 Monergism.com.

All rights reserved under International and Pan-American Copyright Conventions. No part of this text may be reproduced, transmitted, downloaded, decompiled, reverse engineered, or stored in or introduced into any information storage and retrieval system, in any form or by any means, whether electronic or mechanical, now known or hereinafter invented, without the express written permission of Monergism Books.

ISBN
Paperback 978-1-64863-129-0

Visit **Monergism.com** for more God glorifying and Christ exalting free ebooks and resources.

CONTENTS

Part I: The Chief of Sinners Saved 1

Part II: God's Regard for His Own Glory 13

Part III: The Fruits of Converting Grace..30

PART I

THE CHIEF OF SINNERS SAVED

This is a faithful saying, and worthy of all acceptation, that Christ Jesus came into the world to save sinners; of whom I am chief.
1 Timothy 1:15

I. Obs. The salvation of sinners was the main design of Christ's coming into the world. II. God often makes the chiefest sinners objects of his choicest mercy.

Regarding the second point, it should be noted that:

1.God has previously extended invitations to such sinners. Look at how sinful they were, as described in Isaiah 1. They were rebels, and rebels against the one who had nurtured them: "I have nourished and brought up children, and they have rebelled against me" (verse 2). In this respect, they were worse than the animals they owned; the dull ox and the stupid donkey were more clever: "The ox knows its owner, and the donkey its master's crib; but Israel does not know, my people do not consider" (verse 3). God calls on heaven and earth to judge them (verse 2). He appeals to men and angels as a jury to give their verdict, whether these people had not been the most ungrateful and disingenuous people in the world. If by "heaven and earth" he meant magistrates and people, as is usually the case in prophetic language, then God is appealing to them to let their own natural consciences and common sense judge between them. He accuses them of being "laden with iniquity" (verse 4). They had such heavy burdens on them that they could not move, or they were burdened like crabapples with sour fruit. They had come from a wicked stock; they had corrupted one another by their society and example, as rotten apples putrefy the sound ones that lie near them.

They were incorrigible even under punishment. God had used the rod again and again, but since there was no reform, he was tired of whipping them: "Why should you be beaten anymore? You will revolt more and more" (verse

5). They were also so completely corrupted that there was no healthy part about them; they had running sores all over them. Both their heads and hearts were affected; corrupt ideas in the former, and corrupt emotions in the latter. If you take it prophetically, the head signifies the chief magistrate, the heart the judges, and the feet the common people. The fire that had burned their cities had not consumed their desires and had not dried up their sins: "Your country is desolate, your cities are burned with fire, strangers devour your land in your presence, and it is desolate, as overthrown by strangers" (verse 7). If it had not been for a small remnant, they would have been as bad as Sodom and Gomorrah (verse 9). Their religious services were impure, vain, and an abomination to God (verse 13). They were a nuisance to him, his soul hated them, he was tired of them (verse 14), for they came into his presence with their bloody, murderous hands.

Yet, even though he rightly accused them of those terrible crimes, he offers them the assurance of forgiveness if they would return to him: "Come now, and let us reason together," verse 18. He is willing to discuss the matter with them, even though one might have thought he would have nothing to do with such a group. God loves to talk to people about the topic of forgiveness, and he loves it when people listen to him speak about it. He wants to convince them to turn away from their sins and towards a good and proper understanding of his mercy. For example, "Turn to him from whom the children of Israel have deeply revolted," Isaiah 31:6. Revolted! That is their sin; deeply, that is the aggravation of it; and because they are also the children of Israel, a people who have received much mercy and witnessed many miracles, there is another aggravation. Yet, turn to him against whom you have sinned. The main objection of someone who repents is, "I have sinned, and I do not know whether God will accept me." Remember, God knows your sin better than you do, yet he kindly calls out to you and promises you as good a reception as if you had never sinned.

So, "They say, if a man divorces his wife, and she goes from him and becomes another man's, can he return to her again? Would not that land be greatly polluted? But you have played the harlot with many lovers; yet return to me," says the Lord, Jeremiah 3:1. Even though you have been an unfaithful woman, and welcomed any and every person into your bed, and have allied yourself with many sins, upon your return, I will accept you. These are the guarantees of God's encouragement.

2. God has given examples of it in Scripture. Adam, the leader of all rebellions of mankind in the world, had the promise of the seed of the woman to break the serpent's head made to him, and in the genealogy of Christ is called

the son of God, Luke 3:38, not only in respect of creation, for so the devil is the son of God, but in a closer relation. Yet all the wickedness that has overflowed the world since the fall originated from him; moreover, Abraham, the father of the faithful, was probably an idolater in Ur of the Chaldees and a worshipper of the sun and fire, as his ancestors were, Josh. 24:2. Yet God made a particular covenant with this man, presented him with a richer act of grace than anyone else in the world had received. The Messiah, the great Redeemer of the world, would come from his seed. This man is set up as the pattern of faith for others, and his bosom seems to be a great receptacle of saints in glory, Luke 16:22, 23. Israel's sins were like a thick cloud, yet this powerful sun melted them: 'I have blotted out your transgressions like a thick cloud, and your sins like a cloud,' Isa. 44:22. A sullen, gloomy morning often ends in a well-composed noon. Manasseh is an excellent example of this doctrine. His story, 2 Chron. 33, portrays him as a black devil, considering all the aggravations of his sins.

(1.) It was against knowledge. He had a pious education under a religious father. Education usually leaves some traces and impressions of religion. No doubt, the instructions his father Hezekiah taught him, and the exemplary holiness he had seen in him, were sometimes awakened in his memory and recoiled upon his conscience.

(2.) His place and station; a king. Sins of kings are like their robes, more scarlet and crimson than the sins of a peasant. Their example usually infects their subjects. As they are not without their attendants in their travels and recreations, so neither in their vices and virtues.

(3.) Restoration of idolatry. Had he found the worship of the host of heaven inherited from his father, and the idols set up to his hand, the continuance of them would have less sin, because of more temptation. But he rebuilt those high places and altars to idols after they had been broken down, ver. 3, and dashed in pieces the reformation his father had accomplished.

(4.) Affronting God to his very face. He sets up his idols, as it were, to taunt God, and built altars in the house of the Lord and in the two courts of his temple, where God had said he would have his name there forever, ver. 4, 5, 7. He brought in all the stars of heaven to share in that worship that was only due to the God of heaven. What! Could he find no other place for his idols but in the very temple of God? Must God be ousted from his house to make room for Baal?

(6.) Pact with the devil. He used sorcery and witchcraft, and dealt with a familiar spirit, verse 6. Moreover, he had acquaintance with more than one devil, and dealt with familiar spirits and wizards, in the plural number.

(7.) Others' sins. He not only led the people by his example but also compelled them through his commands. "So Manasseh made Judah and the inhabitants of Jerusalem to err and to do worse than the heathen God had rooted out," 2 Chronicles 33:9, to make room for them. By doing so, he incurred the guilt of the entire nation on himself.

(8.) Refusal to heed warnings: "God spoke to him and his people, but they would not listen or change their ways," 2 Kings 21:10.

(9.) Perseverance in wrongdoing. He became king at a young age of twelve years, verse 1. It is uncertain how long he persisted in this sin. Torniellus thinks fifteen years; Bellarmine, twenty-seven; Kimchi, fifty years, counting only five years of his life after his restoration. What a multitude of sins, and what aggravations of them, were there in this man! Yet, God was entreated, verse 19.

3. The lineage from which Christ came seems to suggest this: God could have kept the ancestry from which Christ descended pure and untainted by any notorious sins, but we find that even among them, there were sins of a serious nature. The women mentioned in Christ's genealogy are all noted in scripture for their immoral behavior, as in Matthew 1:3: Tamar, who committed adultery with Judah, her father-in-law, as recounted in Genesis 28; Rahab, mentioned in verse 5, who was a prostitute in Jericho; Ruth, also mentioned in verse 5, a Gentile and a Moabitess, whose genealogy traced back to Lot's son through incest with his own daughter; Bathsheba, mentioned in verse 6, who committed adultery with David. God chose these repentant sinners, from whom Christ was to come, so that the worst of sinners might not be afraid to come to Him.

But was David, whose son is called our Saviour, much better? It is true that he was a man after God's own heart, but he was also notorious for his acts of murder and adultery, with more aggravating circumstances than are usually found in such crimes. As recounted in 2 Samuel 11, Uriah, a godly man who had a sense of the condition of the church and nation, was the victim of David's sinful actions. David not only defiled the bed of a man who was a member of the same church and nation, but he also polluted his own soul with drunkenness and plotted Uriah's death in a sly and treacherous manner, drawing up secret instructions for Joab so that Uriah could be killed. He then made Uriah the carrier of the commission for his own death, all while treating him kindly in his palace. After all this, David showed no remorse when he heard of Uriah's death, but instead shifted the blame to providence. The fact that Christ's lineage was tainted in this way is evidence that repentant sinners, no matter how polluted they were, were welcome to come to Christ. Just as God chose those from whose loins Christ was to come, He would also choose those in whose hearts He would reside.

4. It was Christ's mission in the world to seek and save such kind of people. The first thing he did, while in the manger, was to take some of the Magi, who were astrologers and idolaters, out of the devil's service and bring them into his own, as recorded in Matthew 2:1. When he fled from Herod's cruelty, he chose Egypt, the most idolatrous country in the world, for his sanctuary, a place where the people worshiped oxen, crocodiles, cats, garlic, and all kinds of idols, to show that he often comes to dwell in the darkest souls. The first people he took care to preach to were the sailors, who are usually the most uncivilized and immoral sort of people, as they pick up vices as well as commodities from the nations they trade with, as stated in Matthew 4:13. The inhabitants of those seacoasts are said to sit in darkness, in darkness of sin and ignorance, just as the Egyptians were not able to move around in that thick darkness sent as a plague upon them. And the country, because of the vices of its inhabitants, is called the region and shadow of death, a title that properly belongs to hell itself. The purpose of his coming was to call sinners to repentance. He usually delighted in choosing people who had no merit, such as Matthew, a tax collector, Zacchaeus, an extortionist, and many others like them.

He chose his followers from the devil's crowd, and he was more of a Savior among this sort of people than among all other types of people, for his entire purpose was to get clients out of hell itself. Who was that woman that he went out of his way to convert? She was a harlot, as noted in John 4:18, an idolater, as the Samaritans had a mixed religion, and, because of that, were despised by the Jews. She continued in her adultery at the very time Christ spoke to her, yet he made her a monument of his grace, and not only that, but the first preacher of the gospel to her neighbors, saying, "Is not this the Christ?" in verse 29, and an instrument to lead them to him, saying, "Come, see a man which told me all things," etc. Was anyone more defiled than Mary Magdalene? Seven demons had possessed her, and Christ cast them all out of her. "Now, when Jesus was risen early the first day of the week, he appeared first to Mary Magdalene," Mark 16:9, out of whom he cast seven demons. This lustful devil he turned into a weeping saint.

What was the Canaanite woman who had such a powerful faith given to her? She was from a cursed family, hated by God, driven out of the pleasant land, a dog, not a child; she came as a dog, but returned as a child. Christ made this crab in the wilderness bring forth fruit, even the best that heaven could offer, namely, the fruit of faith; and larger and better bunches of it than at that time sprouted out of any branches of the Jewish vine, so well planted, and so often watered by Christ himself. When he came to act his last part in the world, he saved a thief who was at the gates of hell, ready to be pushed in by the devil. Do you find examples among the Pharisees? No, wretched sinners take heaven by force, while the proud Pharisees lose it through their own righteousness. Scribes and doctors continue to act as devils in power, while harlots begin as saints from the stews, and the thief becomes a convert on the cross.

Since there was only one person whom he converted after he went to heaven, what was he? He was someone who "breathed out slaughters and threatenings against the church," Acts 9:1. Doing so was as common and natural to him as breathing in air and breathing it out again. This man, galloping to hell as fast as his mad rage and passion could carry him, stopped in his career and ordained a preacher of persecution; he gave him as large a commission as he had given any of his favorites, for he made him the chiefest apostle of the Gentiles. What bogs and miry places did Christ drain and make fruitful gardens! What barren and thorny wildernesses did he change into pleasant paradises! He made subjects of vengeance objects of mercy; he told the woman of Samaria, who lived in fornication, that he was the Messiah. "The woman said to him, 'I know that Messiah cometh, which is called Christ': Jesus said to her, 'I that speak unto thee am he,'" John 4:25, which he never revealed to the self-righteous Pharisees, nor indeed in so many words to his disciples, until Peter's confession of him.

5. The commission Christ gave to his apostles was to this purpose. He instructed them to proclaim the promise free to all: "Go into all the world and preach the gospel to every creature," Mark 16:15. Everyone, regardless of their appearance or character, should be offered salvation if they will receive it. The treasures of grace should be opened to them and they should be offered nothing but faith for justification and salvation through a profession of faith.

This commission is illustrated by the parable of a king who commanded his servants to bring in the poor, the maimed, the halt, and the blind, with their wounds, sores, and infirmities about them: Luke 14:21, 23, "Bring in here the poor and the maimed, the halt and the blind." And also go out into the highways and hedges, and those loathsome persons, those dregs of mankind, which you shall find swarming with vermin, and cleaning themselves under every hedge, bring them in. If they object because of their rags and filth, force them to come, that my house may be filled. God wants heaven to be filled with such people when self-righteous persons refuse him. When you come to heaven, to sit down with Abraham, Isaac, and Jacob, you will find many people who were once morally filthy, like these hedge-birds who were naturally so. This kind of compulsion was experienced in the primitive times by the power of the Spirit of grace. Two stage-players, who had mocked the Christian religion in their performances, were converted and became martyrs; one under Diocletian and the other under Julian.

6. The practice of the Spirit after Christ's ascension to lay hold of such persons.

(1.) Some out of the worst families in the world; one out of Herod's: Acts 13:1, 'Now there were in the church that was at Antioch certain prophets and teachers, such as Barnabas, Simeon (called Niger), Lucius of Cyrene, and Manaen, who had been brought up with Herod the tetrarch, and Saul.' Whether it was Herod Antipas, who mocked Christ before Pilate, or Herod Agrippa, who killed James, it is unclear, but it is unlikely that anyone brought up in such a family would have learned principles that were favourable to the Christian religion. Yet, the Holy Spirit called out one person from the family of this wicked prince, not only to make him an object of mercy but also an instrument of it to others. This goes against the usual effect of education, which tends to instil bad principles deeply in one's heart. It is significant that the Holy Spirit takes special notice of the place of Manaen's education, while the families where the others were brought up are not mentioned. Some rough stones were taken out of Nero's palace, including some who served the most abominable tyrant and greatest monster of mankind, who set Rome on fire, played his harp while the flames engulfed the city, and even ripped open his mother's belly to see where he lay. Would any civilised person be a servant to such a devil? Yet, some of this monster's servants became saints: Philip. 4:22, 'All the saints greet you, but especially those who are of Caesar's household.' To hear of saints in Nero's family is as much a wonder as to hear of saints in hell. God had promised his grace to Egypt, the most idolatrous country, and there God wanted an altar built: 'In that day, five cities in the land of Egypt will speak the language of Canaan and swear allegiance to the Lord of hosts. In that day, there will be an altar to the Lord in the heart of Egypt,' Isa. 19:18–20. The gospel was indeed renowned in Egypt, both at the Christian school in Alexandria and through many famous luminaries.

(2.) Some of the worst vices. The Ephesians were as bad as any, such that Paul calls them darkness itself; 'For you were once darkness,' Eph. 5:8. They were not only covered in darkness, but they had changed into the very essence of night. They were great idolaters. The temple of Diana, which was worshipped and visited by people from all over Asia and the world, was located in that city: Acts 19:27, 'So that not only this our craft is in danger to be set at nought; but also that the temple of the great goddess Diana should be despised, and her magnificence should be destroyed, whom all Asia and the world worshippeth.' They elevated this statue, which they claimed fell from Jupiter, above Christ, who was preached by Paul. They were involved in magic and other diabolical arts, yet many of them were weaned from their idols and their magic, and were transformed from darkness to light in the Lord. This is more amazing than seeing a black piece of pitch transformed into a clear piece of crystal, or a stone ascending to the nature of a glittering star.

Take a look at another group, in Corinth, who were as immoral as anyone you have ever heard of, 'such were some of you,' 1 Cor. 6:11. After he listed their sins against natural law and made the list so complete that very little could be added, he adds, 'such were some of you.' Not all, but some. 'But you are washed,' etc. Not people like that, but such sins. These people were not only committing a few acts of sin, but they were so habituated to them that they appeared to have been transformed into the very essence of these sins themselves, so that they were the dirt, mud, and rubbish of hell. Yet, you can see how he truly turned devils into angels of light. Well, then, how many flinty rocks has God dissolved into a stream of tears! How many hard hearts has he made to bleed and melt! That which is now pure gold was once earthy and polluted.

I will only add this to everything I have said. Great sins can be used by God to prepare some people for their conversion, not in their own nature (that is impossible), but by the wise arrangement of God. Mr Burges illustrates this by saying that, like a child whose coat is only slightly dirty, it is not washed immediately. However, when he falls head over heels in the mud, it is taken off and washed right away. The child might have gone many days with a little dirt, had such an accident not occurred. Peter might have still had his proud and vain nature if he had not fallen so terribly in the denial of his Master; but when he fell into the gutter, it helped his conversion, for that is how Christ calls it: "And when you have turned back, strengthen your brothers," Luke 22:32; it was a new edition of conversion, and you never find him in the same boasting vanity again.

David's fall into the sin of murder and adultery is the cause of the plundering of his soul, which you don't find him so worked up about at other times. He digs all around to the very root: "Behold, I was shaped in iniquity, and in sin did my mother conceive me," Ps. 51:5. This sin had stirred up all the mud in his heart and made him see himself as an abominable creature; therefore, he asks

God to hide his face from his sins, ver. 9. He was so repulsive that he would not let anyone look at him (get all this mud out of my soul); and he prays more earnestly for a new heart and a right spirit. So when a wicked person falls into some serious sin that their conscience scowls at and flogs them for, they look for a shelter, which they never did in all their peaceful wickedness.

II. Why God chooses the greatest sinners, and lets his elect run on so far in sin before he turns them.

1. The greatest sinners have a passive disposition to see their need more than moral or superstitious men because they cannot boast of any self-righteousness. A blameless outward appearance and freedom from the common sins of their time and place often deceives them, causing them to become cold and distant towards Christ. They imagine that Christ cannot but look upon them, even if they never turn towards him. Because they are not steeped in such serious sins as others, their consciences are not disturbed by self-reflection. Therefore, when the law's threats are directed at certain sins, these men wipe their mouths, being untainted by those sins, and vainly boast in their outward appearance. Like the Pharisee, they thank God that they are not sinners of such a scarlet dye and that they perform certain duties. As a result, they continue without seeing the need for a new birth, and this allows the strength of sin to become more condensed and strengthened in them.

Superstitious and formal men are hardly brought to their right minds, partly because of a defect in their reasoning from which those extravagances arise, and partly because those false habits and spirit of error that possess their faculties make them incapable of more noble impressions. Moreover, they are more stubborn in the opinions they have absorbed, which have gained control and command over their souls. Such misguided zeal fortifies men against proposals of grace and binds them in a more obstinate inflexibility to any converting motions. This self-righteous temperament is like an external heat that enters the body, producing a hectic fever that is not easily detected until it becomes incurable. Naturally, it is more difficult to part with self-righteousness than to part with gross sins because it is more deeply rooted in the stock of self-love, a principle that does not depart from us without our very nature. Self-righteousness has more arguments to support it and has a natural conscience, a patron of it, whereas a great sinner is speechless when reproved, and a faithful monitor has a good second and correspondent of natural conscience within a person's own breast. It was not the gross sins of the Jews against the light of nature so much as the establishment of the idol of their own righteousness that hindered them from submitting to the righteousness of God (Romans 10:3).

Christ "came to his own, and his own received him not," John 1:11. Those who seem to have his particular stamp and mark upon them, those whose moral righteousness resembled that of God and who remained undefiled by the common pollutions of the world, did not receive him. Meanwhile, tax collectors and prostitutes got ahead of them and grasped the offers of grace: "Truly, I tell you, the tax collectors and the prostitutes are entering the kingdom of God ahead of you," Mat. 21:31. Just like travellers who have wasted their time in a pub, aware of how the darkness is creeping up on them, hurry on and outstrip those who were many miles on their way, and arrive at their destination before them, these tax collectors and prostitutes, who were far from heaven, reached it before those who, like the young man, were not far from it.

Great sinners are most easily convinced of the notorious wickedness of their lives. They reflect on their terrible crimes against the light of nature, are more inclined to try to escape from the devil's slavery, and are frightened and shaken by their consciences into compliance with the doctrine of redemption. Meanwhile, those who do by nature the things contained in the law are so much a law to themselves that it is challenging to persuade them of the necessity of conforming to another law and giving up this self-law in matters of justification. As metals of the noblest substance are hardest to be polished, so men of the most generous, natural, and moral endowments are more difficult to be argued into a state of Christianity than those of more base conversations. Cassianus speaks very confidently in this case: We frequently see that people who are cold and carnal come to spiritual fervor; we never see this happen with the refined and sensual.

2. To show the insufficiency of nature for a work like conversion, so that people do not worship their own intelligence and power. Changing from acts of sin to moral duties can be accomplished through natural strength and the power of natural conscience; for the very same motives that led to sin, such as education, interest, and profit, may, under different circumstances, lead people to outward morality. But a change to the grace of the opposite is supernatural.

Two things are certain in nature: (1.) Natural inclinations never change, except by some superior power. A lodestone will not stop attracting iron as long as it has that quality. The wolf can never love the lamb, nor the lamb the wolf; everything must act in accordance with its nature; water can only moisten, fire can only burn; similarly, man's corrupt nature, being possessed with an invincible hostility and enmity towards God, will never allow him to comply with God. And a sinner's inclination to sin, being strengthened by the frequency of sinful acts, is just as powerful and natural to him as any qualities are to natural agents; and being stronger than any sympathies in the world, cannot be turned into a contrary channel by a person's own power or the power of any other nature equal to it.

(2.) Nothing can act beyond its own principle and nature. Nothing in the world can elevate itself to a higher rank of being than the one in which nature has placed it. A spark cannot make itself a star, even if it reaches a little towards the heavens. A plant cannot give itself senses, nor can an animal adorn itself with reason, nor can a human make themselves an angel. Thorns cannot produce grapes, nor can thistles produce figs because such fruits are above the nature of those plants. Likewise, our corrupt nature cannot produce grace, which is a fruit beyond it. *Effectus non excedit virtutem suae causae,* grace is more excellent than nature, and therefore cannot be the fruit of nature. It is Christ's conclusion, 'How can you, being evil, speak good things?' Mat. 12:33, 34. Not even the buds and blossoms of words, much less the fruit of actions. They cannot change their nature any more than a viper can remove its poison. Although what I have said is true, there is nothing that people desire more than self-sufficiency and independence from any other power but their own. This temperament is as deeply rooted in human nature as any other false principle. People derive it from their first parents, as the prime legacy bequeathed to their nature. At his fall, the first thing that was discovered in humans was the desire to be like God, independent of him. To counter this principle, God allows his elect, like Lazarus, to lie in the grave until they stink, so that there can be no excuse to attribute their resurrection to their own power. If a putrefied, rotten carcass were brought back to life, it could never be thought that it inspired itself with that active principle. God allows people to go so far into sin that they unman themselves, so that he may proclaim to the world that we are unable to do anything on our own at first towards our recovery without a superior principle. The evidence of this will become clear if we consider,

1. Man's subjection under sin. He is 'sold under sin,' Rom. 7:14, and brought into captivity to 'the law of sin,' ver. 23; the law of sin, meaning that sin seems to have a legal authority over him. And man is not only a slave to one sin, but many: Titus 1:3, 'serving various desires.' Now, when a person is sold under the power of a thousand desires, each of which has absolute control over them and rules them as a sovereign by a law; when a person is bound by a thousand

laws, cords and fetters, and carried where their lords please, against the dictates of their conscience and the force of natural light, can anyone imagine that their own power can rescue them from the strength of these masters that claim such a right to them, and keep such a force upon them, and have so often defeated their own strength when they offered to turn against them?

2. Man's affection to them. They not only serve them, but they serve them, and each of them, with delight and pleasure, Titus 3:3. They were all pleasures as well as desires, friends as well as lords. Will anyone leave their indulgences and such sins that please and flatter their flesh? Will a person ever try to run away from those lords which they serve with affection? They have as much delight in being bound a slave to these desires as the devil has in binding them. Therefore, when you see a person cast away their pleasures, deprive themselves of those pleasures to which their soul was once attached, and walk in paths contrary to their corrupt nature, you may search for the cause anywhere, rather than in nature itself. No piece of dirty muddy clay can form itself into a neat and handsome vessel; no plain piece of timber can fit itself for the building, much less a crooked one; nor can a person who is born blind give themselves eyes.

God deals with people in this case as He did with Abraham. He did not give Isaac when Sarah's womb, in a natural probability, could have borne him. But when her womb was dead, and age had taken away all natural strength of conception, then God gave him. This was so it might be apparent that Isaac was not a child of nature but a child of promise. I have gone into detail on these two topics, which I present more as things that need to be established than as reasons, because these two principles of common honesty and self-sufficiency are the great obstacles to conversion and are natural to most people.

PART II
GOD'S REGARD FOR HIS OWN GLORY

1. The glory of his patience. We wonder when we see a notorious sinner how God can still withhold his thunders and allow his sword to rust in his sheath. And in fact, when such sinners are converted, they themselves marvel that God did not draw his sword and pierce their bowels or shoot one of his arrows into their hearts all this while. But by displaying such forbearance, God shows himself to be truly God, and infinitely superior to such a weak creature as man: "I will not execute the fierceness of mine anger, I will not return to destroy Ephraim; for I am God, and not man," Hosea 11:9. When God had listed their sins before, and they might have expected judgment after hearing the charges, God tells them he would not destroy them, he would not execute them, because he was God. If he were not God, he could not refrain from pouring out just vengeance upon them. Even if a man inherited all the meekness of all the angels and all the men that ever were in the world, he would not be able to bear with patience the excesses and injustices committed in the world in the space of a single day; for only a God, that is, one who is infinitely patient, can bear with them.

Not a sin passed in the world before the coming of Christ in the flesh, but was a commendatory letter of God's forbearance, "To declare his righteousness for the remission of sins that are past, through the forbearance of God," Rom 3:25. And not a sin passed before the coming of Christ into the soul, but gives the same testimony and bears the same record. And the greater number of sins and great sins are passed, the more trophies there are erected to God's longsuffering. The reason why the grace of the gospel appeared so late in the world was to testify God's patience. Our apostle takes notice of this long-suffering towards himself in bearing with such a persecutor: "However, for this cause I obtained mercy, that in me first Jesus Christ might show forth all long-suffering, for a pattern to them which should hereafter believe on him," 1 Tim. 1:16. This was Christ's end in letting him run so far, that he might show forth not a few mites, grains, or ounces of patience, but all longsuffering, longsuffering without measure or weight, by wholesale. And this as a pattern to all ages of the world; ὑποτύπωσιν, for a type: a type is but a shadow in respect of the substance. To show that all the ages of the world should not waste that patience, whereof he had then manifested but a pattern. A pattern, we know, is less than the whole piece of cloth from whence it is cut; and as an essay is but a short taste of a person's skill, and does not discover all their art, as the first miracle Christ wrought, of turning water into wine, as a sample of what power he had, was less than those miracles which succeeded; and the first miracle God wrought in Egypt, in turning Aaron's rod into a serpent, was but a sample of his power which would produce greater wonders; so this patience to Paul was but a little essay of his meekness, a little patience cut off from the whole piece, which should always be dealing out to some sinners or other, and would never be cut wholly out till the world had left being. This sample or pattern was but of the extent of a few years; for Paul was but young, the Scripture terms him a young man, Acts 7:58, about thirty-six years of age, yet he calls it all longsuffering. Ah, Paul! Some since have experienced more of this patience; in some, it has reached not only to thirty, but forty, fifty, or sixty years.

2. Grace. It is partly for the admiration of this grace that God intends the day of judgment. It is a strange thing: 'When he shall come to be glorified in his saints, and to be admired in all them that believe in that day,' 2 Thessalonians 1:10. What, does not Christ have enough glory in heaven with his Father? Will he come on purpose to seek glory from such unworthy creatures as his saints are? What is it that glorifies Christ in them? It is the gracious work he has done in them. The word used is "to be glorified in his saints", which means that they will glorify Christ actively and objectively. Just as creatures glorify the wisdom and power of God by providing material for humans to do so, the work of God in saints provides matter for angels to praise and devils to admire. The apostle uses two words: "glorified", which refers to the work of angels and saints, who will sing his praises for it, as a prince receives the congratulations of all his nobility after a great conquest; "admired", which the devil and the damned will do. Although their malice and condition will not allow them to praise him, his inexpressible love in making such dark souls so beautiful will astonish them.

In this sense, those things under the earth will bow down to the name of Jesus, a Saviour - a name which God gave him at first. "Therefore God has highly exalted him and given him a name that is above every name, so that at the name of Jesus every knee should bow," Philippians 2:9-10. And upon his exaltation, he confirmed in Hebrews 5:9, when he was made perfect, that is, exalted, he became the author of eternal salvation and had the power of saving as well as the name conferred upon him. They shall confess that he is Lord, Philippians 2:11, that is, he acted like a Lord when he prevailed over all the opposition which those great sinners made against him. The whole trial of the saints and the sentence of their blessedness shall be finished before that of the damned, Matthew 25:35-44. This is so that the whole scene of his love and the wonders of the work of faith being laid open might strike them with vast amazement. It is evident that this is the design of Christ to be thus glorified in his grace and power, as seen in the apostle's prayer in verses 11 and 12, that the Thessalonians might be among those Christ should be thus glorified in. Therefore he prays that God would "fulfil all the good pleasure of his goodness," that grace he so pleased and delighted to manifest, and carry on the work of faith with power; "that the name of Christ might be glorified in them" as well as in the rest of his saints. Ordinary conversion is an act of grace; Barnabas so interprets it in Acts 11:21-23, when a great number believed. What an abundance of grace, then, is expended in converting a company of extraordinary sinners!

It is the glory of man to overlook an offence (Proverbs 19:11). This means that it is admirable for someone to have this characteristic. If it is an honour to overlook an offence in general, then the greater the offence and the more of them that a person can overlook, the greater their honour will be, as it shows that they have a stronger and more robust version of this quality. Therefore, it must be even more indicative of God's exceeding grace to forgive many and great sins in humans than to forgive only a few lesser ones.

(1.) The abundance of His grace. This demonstrates that God has more grace in Him than there can be sin in us or in the entire world. He allows some sinners to run up a great debt on His account to show that though they are bankrupt, His grace is not. Even though they have spent all of their resources on their depraved desires, they have not exhausted His treasures, just as the sun is not weakened by the fumes of so many garbage heaps. This was His purpose in giving the moral law: the *finis operis*, or outcome of the law, was to increase sin. But the *finis operantis*, or effect of the law, was to glorify His grace. "Moreover, the law entered that the offence might abound. But where sin abounded, grace did much more abound" (Romans 5:20). When the law of nature was out of print and so smudged that it could hardly be read, God brought the moral law (the equivalent of the law of nature) into the world in a new edition. As a result, sin now has more aggravations, as it is a rebellion against a clearer light and a surge and flood over the mighty barrier of the law that was put in its way. But this was useful to the abundance of His grace, which had more abundant material to work with and a wider field to plant its endless seed in. It ὑπερεπερίσσευσεν, it super-abounded. Grace rose higher than sin and swept it away, just as the rolling tide of the sea rises higher than the river streams and pushes them back with all their dirt and filth. It was mercy in God to create us; it is abundant mercy to make any new creatures after they have forfeited their happiness (1 Peter 1:3), which is according to His abundant mercy (κατὰ τὸ πολὺ). However, it was ὑπερπλεονάζουσα χαρις, overflowing, exceeding abundant, more than full grace, to make such misshapen creatures new creatures (verse 14 of this chapter).

(2.) Freely given grace. No one can imagine that Christ should owe anything to sin, except in punishment, and even less that he should owe something to the worst of sinners. But if Christ only chose people with moral and natural virtues, people might suspect that he was in some way obligated to them, and that the gift of salvation was limited to the endowments of nature and a person's own willpower. However, when he makes no distinction between people with the least and the greatest wrongdoing, and even prefers the most sinful monsters as well as the fairest of nature's children, he builds triumphal arches to his grace on this rubbish, and makes both men and angels gaze admiringly upon these infinitely free mercies when he takes souls full of disease and misery into his arms. By doing so, he demonstrates that the God and Lord of nature is no more obligated to his servant (in regards to the gift of salvation) when she behaves most obediently, than when she rebels against him with the highest hand. And that Christ is completely free from any conditions other than faith, and that he can and will accept the dirt and mud as well as the beauty and varnish of nature if they believe with the same precious faith.

Therefore, it is often God's approach in Scripture, just before offering pardon, to list out the sinner's debts, with their aggravations; to persuade them of their inability to satisfy such a large score, and also to reveal the generosity and vastness of his grace: "But thou hast not called upon me, O Jacob, but thou hast been weary of me, O Israel; thou hast not brought me the small cattle of thy burnt offering, etc., but thou hast made me serve with thy sins, thou hast wearied me with thine iniquities," (Isaiah 43:22–24). When he had informed them how indecently they had dealt with him and had made him a mere slave to their corrupt desires; at the end, when they and no creature else, but would have expected fireballs of wrath to be thrown in their faces; and that God should have dipped his pen in gall and have written their conviction to hell, he dips it in honey and cancels the debt; "I, even I, am he that blotteth out thy transgressions for mine own sake, and will not remember thy sins," verse 25. Could there be any merit here, when the offender, instead of favor, could expect nothing but harshness, as there is nothing but wrongdoing in him?

It is so free that the mercy we misuse, the name we have blasphemed, the name for which we have deserved wrath, opens its mouth with petitions for us; "But I had pity for mine holy name, which the house of Israel had profaned among the heathen whither they went," (Ezekiel 36:21). Not for their sakes. It should be entirely free, for he repeats their profaning of his name four times. This name he would sanctify, i.e., glorify. How? By purifying them from their filthiness, verse 25. His name, while it pleads for them, mentions their demerits, so that grace may appear to be truly gracious and triumph in its own liberality. Our sins against him cannot deserve more than our sufferings for him, and even they are not deserving of the glory that will be revealed, (Romans 8:18).

(3.) Extent of his grace. The mercy of God is called his abundance and exceeding abundance of grace. Now, as there is no end to his holiness, which is his honour, and no limit to his power, there is also no end to his grace, which is his wealth. There is no limit to his resources. Therefore, the worst and greatest sinners are the most suitable for Christ to reveal the abundant wealth of his grace upon. It must show a more vast wealth to forgive great debts and many thousands of talents than to forgive some smaller sins in people of more unblemished behavior. If it were not for the salvation of enormous sinners, we would not know so much about God's wealth; we would not know how wealthy he is or what he is worth. He forgives iniquities for the sake of his reputation, and who can read all the letters of his name or turn over all the pages in the book of mercy? Who can say to his grace, as he does to the sea, "This far shall you come and no farther"?

As the heavens have a vast expanse that, like a great circle, surrounds the earth, which lies in the center like a tiny atom in comparison to that vast body of air and ether, so are our sins compared to the extent of God's mercy. "For as the heavens are higher than the earth, so are my ways higher than your ways, and my thoughts than your thoughts," says the Lord. Men's sins are innumerable, yet they are but ciphers in comparison to the vast sums of grace that are spent every day, for they are finite, but mercy is infinite. Thus, all the sins in the world combined cannot be as extensive as mercy because each of them is finite, and if they are all combined, they still cannot amount to infinity.

The gospel is called "good-will to men"; to all sorts of men, with iniquities, transgressions, and sins of all sorts and sizes. God has stores of mercy lying by him. His treasury is never empty; "Keeps mercy for thousands," Exod. 34:7, in a readiness to deal it upon thousand millions of sins as well as millions of persons. Abraham, Isaac, and Jacob, and all that were before, have not wasted it; and if God were to proclaim his name again, it is the same still, for his name as well as his essence is unchangeable. His grace is no more tied to one sin than it is to one person; he has mercy on whom he will, and his grace can pardon what sins he will; therefore he tells them, Isa. 55:7, that he would multiply pardons. He will have mercy to suit every sin of thine, and a salve for every sore. Though thy sin has its heights and depths, yet he will heap mercy upon mercy, till he makes it overtop thy sin. He will be as good at his merciful arithmetic as thou hast been at thy sinful, if thou dost sincerely repent and reform. Though thou multiply thy sins by thousands, where repentance goes before, remission of sin follows without limitation. When Christ gives the one, he is sure to second it with the other. Though aggravating circumstances be never so many, yet he will multiply his mercies as fast as thou canst the sins thou hast committed.

He has a cleansing virtue and a pardoning grace for all iniquities and transgressions; "And I will cleanse them from all their iniquity, whereby they have sinned against me: and I will pardon all their iniquities, whereby they have sinned, and whereby they have transgressed against me," Jer. 33:8. It is three times repeated, to show that his mercy should be as large as their sin, though there was not a more sinful nation upon the earth than they were. His justifying and sanctifying grace should have as vast an extension, for he would both pardon and cleanse them. Why? Ver. 9, that it might be a name of joy and praise, and an honour to him before all the nations of the earth.

It is so great that self-righteous people complain about it, that such despicable people should be chosen over them, just as the eldest son was angry that his father should show more kindness to the prodigal than to him, Luke 15:28.

(4.) Compassion of his grace. The formal nature of mercy is tenderness, and the natural effect of it is relief. The more miserable the object, the more compassionate human mercy is, and the more willing to help. Now, in God, mercy is not just a quality but a nature. How would the infinite tenderness of His nature be revealed if there were no objects to bring it forth? It would not be recognized as mercy unless it were displayed, nor as tender mercy unless it relieved great and oppressive miseries, for mercy is a quality in humans that cannot be kept at home and locked away in one's own heart, much less in God, in whom it is a nature. The greater the disease, the more compassion is revealed from God, who is so abundantly full of it.

As his purpose in allowing the devil to inflict so many hardships on Job was to show his compassion and tender mercy in relieving him; "You have heard of the patience of Job, and have seen the end of the Lord, that the Lord is very compassionate and merciful," James 5:11; so, in permitting the devil to draw his chosen ones into so many sins, he has the same purpose. And he is more compassionate in helping people under sin than under affliction because the guilt of one sin is a greater misery than the burden of a thousand crosses. If forgiveness is a part of tenderness in people, it is also so in God, who is set, Eph. 4:32, as a pattern of the compassion we are to show to others; "And be ye kind one to another, tender-hearted, forgiving one another, even as God for Christ's sake has forgiven you." The lower a person is brought, the more tender is that mercy that relieves them: "Let thy tender mercies speedily prevent us; for we are brought very low," Ps. 79:8. To visit those who sit in darkness and the shadow of death, and to pardon their sins, is called mercy, with this descriptor of tender; "Through the tender mercy of our God, whereby the day-spring from on high has visited us," Luke 1:77-79. And so it is indeed when he visits the most forsaken sinners.

(5.) Sincerity and pleasure of his grace. Ordinary pardon proceeds from his delight in mercy; "Who is a God like unto thee, that pardons iniquity, and passes by the transgression of the remnant of his heritage. He does not retain his anger forever, because he delights in mercy," Micah 7:18. Therefore, the more of his grace he dispenses upon anyone, the more exceeding delight he has in it because it is a larger effect of that grace. If he were not sincere in it, he would never mention people's sins, which would scare them from him rather than entice them to him. If he were not sincere, he would never change the heart of an enemy and show kindness to them in the very act of enmity; for the first act of grace upon us is quite against our wills. And man is so far from being active in it that he is contrary to it. In the first act of the matter, it is thus with a person, though not in the first moment of that act. But for God to bestow his grace upon us against our wills and when he can expect no appropriate recompense from us, demonstrates the purity of his affection; that when he endured so many contradictions of sinners against himself day by day, yet he is determined to have them, and he does seize upon them, though they struggle and resist in his face and provoke him to cast them off.

It is so much God's delight that it is called by the very name of his glory: "The glory of the Lord shall follow thee," Isaiah 58:8; that is, the mercy of the Lord shall follow them at the very heels. And when they call, it should answer them; and when they cry, He would, like a watchful guardian servant, cry out, "Here I am." So that He never lets a great sinner, when changed into a penitent, wait long for mercy, though He sometimes lets them wait long for a sense of it. This mercy is never so delightful to Him as when it is most glorious, and it is most glorious when it takes hold of the worst sinners. For such black spots which mercy wears upon its face, makes it appear more beautiful.

Christ does not care for staying where He has not opportunities to do great cures, suitable to the vastness of His power, Mark 6:5. When He was in His own country, He could do no great work there, but only laid His hands upon a few sick people. He had not a suitable employment for that glorious power of working miracles. So when people come to Christ with lighter guilt, He has but an under opportunity given Him, and with a kind of disadvantage, to manifest the greatness of His charity. Though He has so much grace and mercy, yet He cannot show more than the nature and exigence of the opportunity will bear; and so His pleasure does not swell so high as otherwise it would do, for little sins, and few sins, are not so fit an object for a grace that would ride in triumph. Free grace is God's darling, which He loves to advance; and it is never more advanced than when it beautifies the most misshapen souls.

3.Power. The Bible describes conversion as a remarkable work and compares it to creation and the resurrection of Christ from the dead.

(1.) Creation. Conversion, when considered simply, is considered by theologians to be a greater work than creation; because in conversion, God exerts more moral power than He did physical power in creation. The world was created by a word; but conversion requires many words and many acts. The heavens are called the work of God's fingers, Psalm 8:3, but the gospel, in its effects, is called the arm of the Lord, Isaiah 53:1. Men only use their arm when a task requires more strength than their fingers possess. Conversion is "the power of God for salvation," and the faith it produces is initiated and completed with power, 2 Thessalonians 1:11. God created the world from nothing, and nothing could contribute objectively to His design, as matter does to a workman's purpose. However, it does not oppose Him, as it is nothing. As soon as God spoke, this nothing gave birth to the sun, moon, stars, earth, trees, flowers, and all the adornments of nature from its barren womb. But sin is actively disobedient, challenges God's commands, disregards His power, fortifies itself against His entry into the heart, and does not give up an inch of ground without a fight. Not only is there a passive unwillingness, but there is also active resistance. His creating power drew the world out of nothing, but His converting power shapes the new creature from something worse than nothing.

Naturally, there is nothing but darkness and confusion in the soul. We have not the slightest spark of divine light, no more than the chaos had, when God commanded light to shine out of that darkness (2 Corinthians 4:6), shone in our hearts. To bring a principle of light into the heart and to set it up despite all the opposition that the devil and a person's own corruption make is greater than creation. As the power of the sun is more seen in scattering the thickest mists that triumph over the earth and mask the face of the heavens than in melting the small clouds compacted of a few vapours, so it must needs argue a greater strength to root out those great sins that were twisted and inlaid with our very nature and become as dear to us as our right eye and right hand than a few sins that have taken no deep root. Every person naturally possesses a hatred of God and opposes everything that would restore God to his right; and since the fall, being filled with a desire of independency that is daily strengthened with new recruits and loath to surrender himself to the power and direction of another, it is a more difficult thing to tame this unruly disposition in a person's heart, I say more difficult than to annihilate him and recreate him again; as it is more easy often for a craftsman to make a new piece of work than to repair and patch up an old one that is out of frame.

Conversion simply is so called: 'Quickened us when we were dead' (Ephesians 2:5). And the power that effects it is the same power that raised Christ from the dead, which was a mighty power that could remove the stone from the grave when Christ lay with all the sins of the world upon him (Ephesians 1:19-20); so the greater the stone is upon them, the greater is God's power to remove it. For if it is the power of God simply to regenerate nature and put a new law into the heart and to qualify the will with a new bias to comply with this law, and to make them that could not endure any thoughts of grace not to endure any thoughts of sin, it is a greater power, surely, to raise a person from that death wherein they have lain thirty or forty years rotten and putrefied in the grave; for if conversion in its nature is creation and resurrection, this must need to be creation and resurrection with an emphasis.

The more severe any illness is and the more deeply rooted it is in the vital organs, and the more complicated it is with other diseases, the greater the power needed to cure it. A disease is easier to treat at the first onset than when it has infected the entire bloodstream and become chronic. Similarly, it is harder to uproot a sin or many sins that have spread their roots deep and withstood many threatening storms, than one that is newly planted.

(3.) Traction or drawing. Drawing implies strength. If conversion is a traction, then more strength is required to draw one who is bound to a post by thick cables than one who is tied only by a few threads, one who has millions of weights upon him than one who has only a few pounds.

(4.) It is the only miracle Christ has left standing in the world and declares Him more to be Christ than anything. When John sent to inquire what He was (Luke 7:20), He returned no other account but a list of His miracles; and the last and greatest of them was the poor being evangelized. It is not to be taken actively as the preaching of the Gospel but passively, that they were transformed by the Gospel and became an evangelized people, conformed to it, for otherwise, it would have no analogy with the other miracles. The deaf heard and the dead were raised, they had not only the exhortations to hear but the effects were worked upon them. So these words not only imply the preaching of the Gospel to them but also the powerful operation of the Gospel within them. It is not as great a work to raise many thousands killed in a battle as to evangelize one dead soul. It is a miracle of power to transform a ravenous wolf into a gentle lamb, a furious lion into a meek dove, a filthy sink into a clear fountain, a stinking weed into a fragrant rose, a toad, or a viper into a man endowed with rational faculties and moral attributes, and so to transform a filthy swine into a king and a priest unto God. Divine power appears glorious in conquests of this nature. It is some strength to polish a rough stone taken out of the quarry and carve it into the statue of a great prince, but it is more to make this statue a living man. God makes children out of worse stones than these, not only to Abraham but also to Himself, even the Gentiles who were considered stones by the Jews and are referred to as stones in Scripture for worshipping idols.

What power must that be which can stop the tide of the sea, and make it suddenly recoil back! What vast power must that be that can change a black cloud into a glorious sun? This and more does God do in conversion. He does not only take smooth pieces of the softest matter, but the ruggedest timber full of knots, to plane and show both his strength and art upon.

4. Wisdom. The work of grace being a new creation, is not only an act of God's power, but of his wisdom, as the natural creation was. As he did in contriving the platform of grace, and bringing Christ upon the stage, so also in particular distributions of it, he acts according to counsel, and that infinite too, even

the counsel of his own will, Eph. 1:11. The apostle, having discussed before (ver. 9) about God's making known the mystery of his will in and through Christ, and (ver. 11) about the dispensation of this grace, in bestowing an inheritance, 'being predestinated according to the purpose of him who works all things according to the counsel of his own will,' does not say God predestinated us according to the counsel of his own will, but refers it to all he had said before, namely, of his making known the mystery of Christ, and their obtaining an inheritance. And ver. 8, speaking before about the pardon of sin in the blood of Christ, according to the riches of God's grace, wherein, he says, 'he has abounded towards us in all wisdom.' As there was an abundance of grace set apart to be dealt out, so there was an abundance of wisdom, even all God's wisdom, employed in the distribution of it. The restoring of God's image requires at least as much wisdom as the first creating of it. And the application of redemption, and bestowing of pardoning and converting grace, is as much an act of God's prudence as the contrivance of it was of his counsel.

Grace, or a gracious person in relation to their grace, is referred to as God's workmanship in Ephesians 2:10, *poema*, not *ergon*—a work of God's art and strength, and an operation of his mind as well as his hand; his poem, not simply a work of omnipotence, but an intellectual spark. A new creation is a fascinating piece of divine art, fashioned by God's wisdom to showcase the excellence of the creator, just as a poem is, by a person's reason and imagination, to publish the cleverness and abilities of the composer. It is a great skill of a craftsman, with a combination of a few sands and ashes, by his breath to inflate such a clear and transparent body as glass and make various vessels of it for several purposes. It is not only his breath that does it, for other people have breath as well as he; but it is breath managed by art. And isn't it a marvellous skill in God to make a muddy soul so pure and crystalline suddenly, to endow an irrational creature with a divine nature, and by a powerful word to create such a beautiful model as a new creation!

The more complex and difficult any task is, the more impressive a person's capability is in accomplishing it. The more severe the wound, the more honourable the surgeon's skill in the cure. Christ's healing of a soul that is at the point of death, and given up for lost by everyone, shows more of his art than restoring an ordinary sinner. Our apostle acknowledges the wisdom of God in his own conversion here; for when he relates the story of it, he breaks out into an Hallelujah, and sends up a volley of praises to God for the grace he has received. And in that doxology, he emphasizes the wisdom of God: 'Now to the King eternal, immortal, invisible, the only wise God, be honour and glory forever and ever,' ver. 17. Only wise God; only, which he does not add to any other attribute he there gives him.

This wisdom appears, (1.) In the subjects he chooses. We will go no further than the example in our text. Our apostle seems to be a man full of heat and zeal. And the church had already felt the pain of his activity, so much so that they were afraid to approach him after his change, or to allow him into their company, believing that his anger was not changed, but concealed, and he who was an open persecutor had turned a trapper, Acts 9:26. No one can express better than he does himself how much of a lion he was: "Many of the saints I shut up in prison, having received authority from the chief priests, and when they were put to death, I gave my voice against them. And I punished them often in every synagogue, and compelled them to blaspheme; and being exceedingly mad against them, I persecuted them even unto strange cities," Acts 26:10, 11. He also appears to have been a man of high and ambitious spirit. This persecution was probably done so vigorously by him to gain favor with the chief priests, and as a means to step into a higher position, for which he was gifted with intelligence and knowledge, and would not lack enthusiasm and hard work to achieve it. He seems to have been of a proud spirit, by the temptation which he faced: "Lest I should be exalted above measure," 2 Cor. 12:7. He says it twice in that verse, indicating that his natural disposition led him to be lifted up with any excellence he had; and usually God directs his battery to beat down what is the sin of our constitution.

He was a man of a very honest mind and was eager to follow every point his conscience directed him to; for what he did against Christ, he did according to the dictates of his conscience, as then informed: "I verily thought with myself," Acts 26:9, i.e. in my conscience, "that I ought," not that I might, but that it was his duty. His error commanded with the same power that truth does where it reigns. Now it shows the wisdom of God to lay hold of this man who was thus tempered, who had the honesty to obey the dictates of a rightly-informed conscience, as well as those of an erroneous one; zeal to execute them, and height of spirit to preserve his activity from being blunted by any opposition, and intelligence and prudence for the management of all these. I say, to turn these emotions and excellencies to run in a heavenly channel, and to guide this natural passion and heat for the service and advancement of that interest which before he tried to destroy, and for the propagation of that gospel which before he persecuted, is an effect of a wonderful wisdom; as it is a rider's skill to order the mettle of a headstrong horse for his own use to carry him on his journey.

(2.) This wisdom appears in the timing. Just as human wisdom involves choosing the right time to act as well as devising plans, so too does God's wisdom. He seizes the most opportune moments to bring his wonderful providences onto the stage. He has appointed times to deliver his church from her enemies (Psalm 102:13) and also to save every individual soul that he intends to make a member of his church from the devil. He waits for the most appropriate time to reveal his grace: "Therefore the Lord waits to be gracious to you, and therefore he exalts himself to show mercy to you, for the Lord is a God of justice" (Isaiah 30:18). Why? Because the Lord is a God of wisdom, and he times things for the best possible outcomes for both his glory and the sinner's good. His timing of his grace was excellent in the conversion of Paul.

[1.] With regard to himself, there could not have been a more fitting time to glorify his grace than when Paul was almost at the end of his rope; almost committing the sin against the Holy Spirit. If he had gained just a little more knowledge and acted out of malice instead of ignorance, he would have been lost forever. But he received mercy because he did it ignorantly, as it says in verse 13. As I mentioned earlier, he followed the dictates of his conscience, for if he had possessed knowledge commensurate with his rage, it would have been the unpardonable sin. Christ allowed him to run to the edge of hell before taking hold of him.

[2.] In respect of others. He was converted at a time when he went as full of madness as a toad of poison to spit it out against the poor Christians at Damascus, armed with all the power and credential letters the high priest could give him, who, without question, promised himself much from his industry. And when he was almost at his journey's end, ready to execute his commission, "And as he journeyed, he came near Damascus," Acts 9:3, about half a mile from the city, as Gulielmus Tyrius thinks, at this very time Christ grapples with him and overcomes all his mad principles, secures Paul from hell and his disciples from their fears of him. Behold the nature of this lion changed just as he was going to fasten upon his prey. Christ might have converted Paul sooner, either when Paul had heard of some of his miracles, for perhaps Paul was resident at Jerusalem at the time of Christ's preaching in Judea, for he was brought up in Jerusalem at the feet of Gamaliel, Acts 22:3, who was one of the council, Acts 5:24. He might have converted him when he heard Stephen make that elegant and convincing oration in his own defence, Acts 7, or when he saw Stephen's constancy, patience, and charity in his suffering, which might have somewhat startled a moral man as Paul was and made him look about him.

But Christ omits doing it at all these opportunities and suffers him to kick against the pricks of miracles, admonitions, and arguments of Stephen and others, yet has his eye upon him all along in a special manner, Acts 7:58. He is named there when none else are: "And the witnesses laid their clothes at a young man's feet, named Saul." And "Saul was consenting to his death," Acts 8:1. Was there none else that had a hand in it? The Spirit of God takes special notice of Saul here. He runs in God's mind, yet God would not stop his fury: "As for Saul, he made havoc of the church," Acts 8:3. Did nobody else show as much zeal and cruelty as Saul? Surely he must have some instrument with him. Yet we hear none named but Saul, and "Saul yet breathing," etc., Acts 9:1, yet, as much as to say, he shall not do so long. I shall have a fit time to meet with him presently.

And was it not a suitable time, when the devil hoped to defeat the Christians by him, when the high priests were certain of success from this man's zealous fervour, when the church was filled with fears of him? But Christ sent the devil slinking away for the loss of such an active instrument, frustrated all the expectations of the high priests, and calmed all the stormy fears of his disciples; for Christ first set him preaching at Damascus in the synagogues which were to assist him in his cruel design: 'And immediately he preached Christ in the synagogues, that he is the Son of God, and increased the more in strength, and confounded the Jews who dwelt at Damascus, proving that this is the very Christ,' Acts 9:20-22.

Did not Christ show himself to be a God of judgment here? He sat watching in heaven for this season to turn Paul with the greatest advantage. His wisdom serves many purposes at once, and killed so many birds with one stone. He struck dead at one blow Paul's sin, his people's fears, the high priests' expectations, and the devil's hopes. He triumphs over his enemies, secures his friends, saves Paul's soul, and promotes his interest through him; he disappoints the devil of his expectations, and hell of her longing.

(3.) This wisdom appears to maintain the credibility of Christ's death. The great excellence of Christ's sacrifice, which surpasses the sacrifices under the law, is that it perfectly atones for all sins. It first satisfies God, and then calms the conscience, which they could not do, as there was still a sense of sin after those sacrifices, as stated in Hebrews 10:1-2. The agreement of the covenant of grace that God makes with his people is based on this sacrifice, "This is the covenant

I will make with them, and their sins and iniquities I will remember no more," as mentioned in Hebrews 10:16-17. "Now where remission of these is, there is no more offering for sin," verse 18. This covenant applies not only to minor sins, as there is no limitation, but major sins are included as well. Therefore, Christ made satisfaction for great sins; otherwise, if ever they are forgiven, there must be another sacrifice, either of himself or some other, which the apostle claims there need not be on the basis of this covenant, because this sacrifice was complete. Otherwise, there would be a remembrance of sin. As the covenant implied the completeness of Christ's satisfaction, so the continuous fulfilment or application of the agreement of the covenant implies the perpetual favour and force of this sacrifice.

And, indeed, when God delivered him up, he intended it for the greatest sins: "He was delivered for our offences," as stated in Romans 4:25, παραπτωματα, which signifies not stumbling, but falling. It denotes not a light, but a significant transgression. Now, if Christ's death is not satisfactory for significant debts, then Christ must be too weak to fulfil what God intended through him, and thus infinite wisdom was frustrated in its intention, which cannot and ought not to be imagined. Therefore, God takes the greatest sinners to demonstrate the magnitude of Christ's sacrifice.

[1.] First, the value of this sacrifice. If God should only accept people with lesser guilt, Christ's death would be suspected to be too small a ransom for monstrous crimes; and that his treasure was enough to pay off smaller debts, but insufficient to discharge greater debts; which would not have been a suitable design for the grandeur of Christ, or the boundlessness of the mercy God proclaims in his word. But now, the conversion of giant-like sinners gives credit to the atonement which Christ made, and is a great renewed approval of the infinite value of it, and its equivalence to God's demands; for it has some similarity to the resurrection of Christ, which was God's general discharge to Christ, to show the sufficiency of his payment. And the justification of every sinner is a part of that discharge given to Christ at his resurrection; 'Raised again for our justification,' Rom. 4:25; and a specific discharge to Christ for that particular soul he had the responsibility of from his Father.

All the power that works in the initial creation of grace or the progress of regeneration bears some proportion to the acquitting and approving power manifested in Christ's resurrection. "And what is the exceeding greatness of his power to us-ward who believe, according to the working of his mighty power, which he wrought in Christ, when he raised him from the dead," Ephesians

1:19-20. In verses 17 and 18, the apostle prays for the continuation of the work of grace and regeneration that has begun in them, so that they may more clearly understand that power which worked in Christ, namely, that approving power of what Christ has done, which he exerts daily in conversion and its effects. For by raising any soul from death in sin, God shows the particular value of Christ's blood for that soul, just as he demonstrated the general fullness of that satisfaction in raising Christ. And he will continue to do this until the end of the world, "raised us up together with Christ;" "kindness through Christ Jesus," Ephesians 2:6-7. All of his grace in all ages, even until the end of the world, shall flow through this channel to put credit and honour upon Christ. The greater the sin that is pardoned, and the greater the sinner who is converted, the more it shows the sufficiency of the price Christ paid.

The virtue of this sacrifice is that he is a "priest for ever," Hebrews 7:17, and therefore, the virtue as well as the value of his sacrifice remains forever. He has "obtained an eternal redemption," Hebrews 9:12, that is, a redemption of eternal efficacy. As long as men receive any venom from the fiery serpent, they may be healed by the antitype of the brazen one, even though it has been so many years since he was lifted up. And those who were stung all over, as well as those who are bitten but in one part, may draw virtue from him as diffusive as their sin by believingly looking upon him.

Now the new conversion of men of extraordinary guilt proclaims to the world that the fountain of his blood is inexhaustible; that the virtue of it is not spent and drained, though so much has been drawn out of it for these five thousand years and upwards, for the cleansing of sins past before his coming, and sins since his death. This evidences that his priesthood now is of as much efficacy as his sufferings on earth were valuable; and that his merit is as much in virtue above our iniquity, as his person is in excellency above our nothingness. He can wash the tawny American, as well as the moral heathen; and make the black Ethiopian as white as the most virtuous philosopher. God fastens upon the worst of men sometimes, to adorn the cross of Christ; and makes them eminent testimonies of the power of Christ's death: 'He made his grave with the wicked,' Isa. 53:9. Heb. 'He shall give the wicked (not grave), and the rich in his death.' God shall make man, wallowing in sinful pleasures, tied to the blandishments and profits of the world, to come to Christ, and comply with him, to be standing testimonies in all ages of the virtue of his sufferings.

(4.) For the fruitfulness of this grace in the converts themselves. The most rugged souls prove most eminent in grace upon their conversion, as the most orient diamonds in India, which are naturally more rough, are most bright and sparkling when cut and smoothed. Men usually sprout up in stature after shattering agues.

PART III
THE FRUITS OF CONVERTING GRACE

1. A sense of the sovereignty of grace in conversion will first increase thankfulness. Converts only are fit to show forth the praises of Christ: 'That you should show forth the praises of him who has called you out of darkness into his marvellous light,' 1 Peter 2:9; virtues of Christ. The end why God sets men at liberty from prisons and dungeons, and from fear of death and condemnation for great sins, is, that they may be fitted, and gain a convenient standing, to publish to the world the virtues of him; i.e. the mercy, meekness, patience, bounty, truth, and other royal perfections of Christ.

Men at their first conversion receive the grace of God with astonishment; for it is an amazing light, 1 Peter 2:9, most amazing at the first appearance of it; as the northern nations, that want the sun for some months in the winter, are ready to deify it when it appears in their horizon; for the thickness of the foregoing darkness makes the lustre of the sun more admirable. But suppose a man had been all his lifetime like a mole underground, and had never seen so much as the light of a candle, and had a view of that weak light at a distance, how would he admire it when he compares it with his former darkness? But if he should be brought further to behold the moon with its train of stars, his amazement would increase with the light. But let this person behold the sun, be touched with its warm beams, and enjoy the pleasure of seeing those rarities which the sun discovers, he will bless himself, adore it, and embrace that person that led him to enjoy such a benefit. And the darkness he sat in before will endear the present splendour to him, swell up such a spring-tide of astonishment, as that there shall be no more spirit in him. God lets men sit long in the shadow of death, and run to the utmost of sin before he stops them, that their danger may enhance their deliverance.

We admire more when we are pulled out of danger than when we are prevented from running into it. A criminal will be more thankful for a pardon when it comes just as he is about to be executed. If there are degrees of harmony in heaven, undoubtedly the converted thief on the cross sings louder notes than others, because he had little time to do it on earth, and his obligations are greater, as Christ took him in his arms when he was hanging over hell.

When Paul wrote this letter to Timothy, he was about 55 years old, and yet those 20 years since his conversion had not stifled his admiration nor dampened his gratitude for the converting grace. Consider this chapter: "And I thank Christ Jesus our Lord, who has enabled me, that he counted me faithful, putting me into the ministry; who was before a blasphemer and a persecutor and an insolent opponent," verse 12, 13. I thank Christ Jesus our Lord. He appears to set his sin and God's mercy against each other. I was insolent, but I received mercy. I was a blasphemer, but I received, etc. I—mercy. Who would have thought that out of all people he should have passed over me, while he had chosen this or that polished Pharisee, this or that doctor of morality? But that he should ignore them and set his sights on me, so insolent, such a blasphemer, such a persecutor! A great sinner, when he reflects on his sin, wonders that a target was not made of him. You will not find any apostle giving such epithets to the grace of God as our apostle did; none so seraphic in his admiring expressions. Riches of grace, exceeding riches of grace, abundant grace, riches of glory, unsearchable riches of grace. He never speaks of grace without emphasis. Single grace and single mercy would not satisfy him.

2. Love and affection. Mary Magdalene, from whom Christ had cast out seven devils, was one of the earliest to show her love by bestowing spices on the dead body of her Saviour. The fire of grace cannot be stifled and will break out in glory to God. This is such a grace that man in innocence could not have exercised in such a height, because now the sinner is not only unworthy of pardon in his own sight, but also worthy of the greatest hatred and punishment. You scarcely find yourselves possessed with greater affection for anyone than those who have been instruments to free you from your sinful fetters. How often do you bless them, could pull out your eyes for them, and think all ways too little to manifest the sense of your obligations to them! And does the instrument carry away all? Surely God has the greatest sacrifice of affection when the convert considers that His powerful grace was the principal agent to draw him out of this spiritual mire. As when a present is sent to you, you show a courtesy to the servant, but the chief part of your kindness is devoted to the master who sent him. What flames of love, raptures of joy, transports of affection, and boilings of courage for God in a young convert! The soul is most courageous for God at

first conversion because it is then most filled with comforts and is so struck into amazement at the marvellous light which darts upon him that he is ambitious to be a martyr for God presently: "After you were illuminated, you endured a great fight of afflictions," Heb. 10:32. Grace is not only attended with afflictions, but also bestows courage upon a convert to endure them. The soul then thinks it is able to undergo anything for God, who has bestowed so much grace upon it.

A Christian has the greatest love for Christ at the first turning to Him, for since the horror of all his sins and the natural ugliness and deformity of that which he has served so long come with a full sense upon him, and since the admirable excellency of Christ shines upon him, which is a sight he was never acquainted with before, the greatness of the danger he was in, and the incomparable love which beams upon him from his believing a Saviour, fills his affection with full sails. Thus, men who have been tossed in a dangerous tempest, afflicted with the darkness of the night as well as their danger, rejoice and welcome the rising sun in the morning, which dispels their tumultuous fears, as well as those gloomy shadows.

God permits a person's sin to abound, so that their love may abound even more after they receive forgiveness: "Therefore, I tell you, her many sins have been forgiven—as her great love has shown. But whoever has been forgiven little loves little" (Luke 7:47). In other words, love is a consequence of forgiveness, not the cause of it. This interpretation is more reasonable and in line with the following words: "But whoever has been forgiven little loves little." It makes sense that where there are greater mercies, there should be greater returns of affection. Forgiveness of sins is the greatest evidence of God's love, and should therefore be the greatest incentive of ours. In fact, Jesus never appears more beautiful to a repentant sinner than when great judgments are removed or great sins are forgiven: "In that day the Branch of the Lord will be beautiful and glorious, and the fruit of the land will be the pride and glory of the survivors in Israel" (Isaiah 4:2). In that day! In what day? After great judgments (Isaiah 3:1-4) and after purging away great filth (Isaiah 4:4). Jesus appears most lovely when He comes with the fruit of grace, with the sanctifying juice of His blood, like a ripe bunch of grapes that looks pleasantly to a thirsty traveller's eye. This convert, Paul, was more affectionate to Christ than any of the other apostles. When he could not look upon Jesus, he was enamoured with His name, delighting to express it no less than five hundred times in his epistles, as some have counted. This was more, proportionally, than Peter, James, and John did in what they wrote.

As for service and obedience, such people will endeavour to redeem the time, because their former days have been so evil, and recover those advantages of service that they lost by a course of sin. They will labour so that the largeness of their sin may be answered by an extension of their zeal. Such people will be almost as ashamed to do common service as they are now ashamed of their scarlet sins. As people, the further they go backward, the greater leap they usually take forward. Grace instructs people in holiness out of gratitude. The grace of God "teaches us to say 'No' to ungodliness and worldly passions, and to live self-controlled, upright and godly lives in this present age" (Titus 2:12). Grace teaches us. The greater the grace, the more pressing the instruction, and as it increases gratitude, it increases service.

That Peter, who had been so guilty in denying his Master, and adding perjury to his faithlessness, was as active in service as he had been in apostasy. He laid the first stone of the Christian church among the Jews after Christ's ascension; he preached the first sermon to them, and charged them home with his Master's murder, Acts 2. He was also the spokesperson in all business described in the first six chapters of the Acts. He also laid the first foundation of the Gentile church; for God in a vision revealed to him the calling of the Gentiles, passing by all the other apostles, to whom it was not known but by Peter's report:* 'Men and brethren, you know how that a good while ago God made choice among us, that the Gentiles by my mouth should hear the word of the gospel, and believe,' Acts 15:7. A good while ago, which refers to the time, Mat. 16:18, when Christ said, 'Upon this rock will I build my church.' He was chosen by God for this purpose, i.e. separated from the rest of the apostles, and adorned with this privilege. Great sins did not make Christ change his resolution.

Never an apostle who had been brought up under Christ's wing was as active an instrument as this Paul, who had been such a bitter enemy. He 'laboured more abundantly than all,' 1 Cor. 15:10. In matters of obedience, he would not ask advice of flesh and blood: 'Immediately I conferred not with flesh and blood,' Gal. 1:16. He was quick in his obedience. He had sought to weaken Christ's kingdom; he now endeavours to enlist men in his service. He had breathed out threats; he now breathes out affections. He could even spend and be spent for the interests of his Saviour. And usually, we find converted souls most active in the exercise of that grace, which is most contrary to that which was their beloved sin.

4. Humility and self-emptying. Christ "chose the foolish things of the world to confound the wise, and the weak things of the world to confound the things

that are mighty," 1 Cor. 1:26-27, so that nothing should be attributed to their worth and dignity, but to his grace and mercy. If the gospel were only revealed to the wise, they would consider it more as a discovery made by the optics of their own reason. And if God only bestowed his grace upon men of unblemished conduct, they would consider it a debt that God was obliged to pay them rather than a free act of grace. As God reveals knowledge to the simplest, Mat. 11:25, so he manifests grace to the greatest sinners. And as Christ blessed his Father for that, so undoubtedly he returns the same thanks for this. Such great sinners receive all from God and have more reason to hang their heads. Others may sometimes cast many loving looks at their own righteousness and, like Nebuchadnezzar, boast, "This is the Babylon which I have built"; and brag about their good deeds and freedom from the common pollutions of the world.

But those who have fallen over head and ears in the mire and are dirty all over have no reason to boast. God did not find them, but made them worthy. They brought nothing but dirt and rags that were not worthy of washing. Only God would pick glory out of their worthlessness for his own grace. Such people are aware that God was not their debtor, but they his, and that there was nothing in them to oblige God to bestow even the slightest bit of mercy upon them.

Therefore, we do not find any of these monstrous sinners in Scripture ascribing their conversion to their own strength or merit. As no apostle was as God-glorifying, none was as self-deprecating as Paul. Though he was the greatest apostle, he considers himself less than the least of all saints: Ephesians 3:8, 'To me, the very least of all saints, this grace was given.' Surely he could have put himself on an equal footing with the least, which would have been great humility, but he is even more humble, less than the least, less even than the one who was only fit to be a doorkeeper in the house of God. And he considers himself unworthy not only of the office of an apostle but of the very name; 'not fit to be called an apostle' 1 Corinthians 15:9. And why? Because of his former sin; 'because I persecuted the church of God.' The memory of his great sin before his conversion kept him humble. And in verse 10, when he had boasted of his abundant labour, he quickly checks himself, 'Yet not I, but the grace of God.' He attributes his very existence as a Christian, as well as his actions, to the same cause, the grace of God; 'By the grace of God, I am what I am.' So, Galatians 1:16, how does Paul attribute grace; 'was pleased to reveal,' revelation, not acquisition.

When people are first transferred from darkness to the kingdom of Christ and start to truly know Christ, the ways of their former ignorance are very bitter and strange to them. The very disproportion and unsuitability of them to the sweetness of that grace which they now taste from the hand of Jesus is an offense to them and detestable to their thoughts. Therefore, the more a person has sinned before returning to God, the more they see the vileness of their own nature and therefore the more they hate themselves: 'Then you will remember your evil ways and wicked deeds, and you will loathe yourselves for your sins and detestable practices,' Ezekiel 36:31. When? In verse 29, when God had fulfilled the promise of saving them from all their uncleanness. They will remember with abhorrence what was theirs, sin, and will enjoy what is purely God's. The time of forgiving great sins is the time of great self-loathing; such people prove to be the holiest because they have experienced more of the evil of sin.

Such people are ashamed of their sins, not only at the moment of their conversion, but also afterwards, every time they remember them: 'What benefit did you reap at that time from the things you are now ashamed of? Those things result in death!' Romans 6:21. At the time when Paul wrote to them, the shame of their sins clung to them, even though they had been converted before. The more they grew in their experiential knowledge of God and His goodness, the more a holy shame for sins committed in their natural state was stirred in their consciences, and they could not help but blush every time they considered how unclean they had been towards God. The greater the shame, the greater the hatred of the occasion of that shame, and the more careful the watchfulness against it. For instance, a person who has stumbled or made an oversight and fallen into some ditch, when he travels that way again, cannot help but remember what a mess he was in and will be watchful lest he meet with the same mishap.

Whose heart was more melted by mercy than Mary Magdalene's? All the Pharisees that Christ converted never rained such showers of tears. How she used all her instruments of sin to be servants to her repentance! Her eyes, which had inflamed so many hearts, been snares to catch men, she makes the conduits to convey her penitential tears to her Saviour's feet. Her hair, which had consumed so much time in the pursuit of beautiful hairstyles, she uses as a towel to wipe them. The ointment she had used to adorn herself and gratify the senses of her lovers, she pours out to embalm her Lord. Her lusts would have no more of her best things, but her Saviour would have all. She would keep them not so much for her own use, as for His.

Faith and dependence. (1.) At present, in the instant of the first act of faith. Great sins make us appear in the court of justification, in the form of an ungodly person, with a naked faith, when we have nothing to merit it, but much to deserve the opposite: 'Believes on him that justifies the ungodly,' Rom. 4:5. The more ungodly, the more elevated is that faith which grasps onto God. Thomas's unbelief was very dark, for he had refused to believe all the testimonies of the disciples concerning Christ's resurrection; but when he was aware of his crime, and kindly dealt with by his Saviour, he puts forth a stronger act of faith than any of the rest: 'My Lord, and my God,' John 20:28. His faith was not content with a single my; he gives him more honourable titles, and his heart grasps him more closely and affectionately than any of the rest.

The man that was born blind, and healed by Christ, acknowledges him, demonstrates some faith before the Pharisees: 'If this man were not of God, he could do nothing,' John 9:33; and he said, 'I believe,' ver. 39, and he worshipped him. But when Christ comes to talk with him particularly, verses 36-38, he believes. When Christ comes to talk with a great sinner, one that has had incurable diseases, he exerts a stronger faith than others. It is then, Lord, I believe, and it is a faith accompanied with adoration.

(2.) In following occasions. Forgiving such great sins, and converting such great sinners, is the best reference letter Christ brings with him from heaven. People naturally would hardly believe for his own sake, but for the sake of his work, because they are more led by sight than faith. Christ knew this, when he tells his disciples to believe him for the sake of the works he did, and that they should be unanimous in this work of grace, as well as in other works: 'Believe me that I am in the Father and the Father is in me, or else believe me for the sake of the works themselves,' John 14:11. Therefore, those who have experienced this transforming grace, if they waver and doubt afterward, they give the greatest insult to Christ.

Their unbelief is not only against his person, but against his work too. He has much more reason to say to them than he did to his disciples, 'How long shall I be with you,' &c., Mat. 17:17: why should I stay to do such great works as these, and cannot be believed? Such great sins forgiven and escaped, make people hold onto Christ more tightly afterward. Like a man who has recently escaped from a deep lake, which was infested with many snakes, crocodiles, and venomous creatures, and has no refuge to protect him from their fury except by hanging onto a small branch; when he looks down at them and sees them gaping at him, ready to devour him if he were within their reach, he would summon all his strength to hold onto that branch. In that day, the branch of the Lord will also be beautiful and glorious.

Certainly, when the soul went out to Christ in such a desperate condition, burdened with guilt and discouragement, and decided to trust in Him no matter what, and found success, it was the boldest venture which Scripture often refers to as boldness, and the greatest encouragement to come to Christ on any occasion thereafter. This first act of faith is of such noble and generous quality that it is considered as the model for all subsequent acts of faith: "We have come to share in Christ, if indeed we hold our original conviction firmly to the very end" (Hebrews 3:14). The original conviction refers to the primary act of faith, which is the principal act of confidence. Although there is greater strength in the habit of faith after conversion, the first exercise of faith in Christ is the boldest and most vigorous because it was for the purpose of saving one's life when the soul saw no way to recover except in Christ, and it was the most noble when under the discouragement of such mountains of guilt.

It also gave Christ the greatest honour, for it was an act of greater confidence in Him than any subsequent act could be. If you put forth such a high and daring act of faith when all your sins were surrounding you, and you had neither a Hur nor an Aaron to hold up your hands, with much more confidence may you come to Him now, since you have seen how successful your first faith was. So, when temptations assail you, and the devil with all his black legions surrounds you, you are not in a worse condition than you were at first when all your sins not only besieged you but possessed you. A soul that acted in faith when the devil had all the strongholds in the worst condition may rightly say, "Now it is just a matter of starting out and exercising the power of that first faith."

(3.) In the case of corruption and uncontrolled sins as well. I have great corruptions, but the power which raised Christ also raised me when I had even greater burdens that had even wearied God himself, and now when I have fewer, though they are still too great, should I give up on that power that worked greater miracles for me and threw away my gravestones when I was unable to move myself?

(4.) So, in the case of feeling abandoned by God, I will take a chance and go to him, even if he scowls and strikes; because I am certain that I went to him once when I was his absolute sworn enemy, and he had no greater foe in the world than me, and he welcomed me. I am not worse now than I was at that time, for I love him and would do all that I can to please him; therefore, I will boldly enter into his presence now and test the success of my first faith. The faith of such individuals is typically more generous because they have less of the principle of reason to support it. It is like that of Abraham's, believing "in hope against hope," Rom. 4:18. It is a faith against the strong opposition of high and mighty sins, which may frighten a person from such acts of faith, and create a lack of confidence in the promises of God in the soul. God receives no more glory from the faith of any individual than from that of the greatest sinner who repents.

7. Fear and reverence. Such a person will never despise the riches of that goodness and patience which has been shown to him, Rom. 2:4, because it has led him to repentance; and he will not provoke that goodness, which is leading him to the enjoyment of all the fruits of repentance, to reject him: 'There is forgiveness with you,' says David, 'that you may be revered,' or worshipped, Ps. 130:4. If God were to mark every iniquity with death, who could stand in his presence or have any hope of being heard? But because he is a God of forgiveness, he is revered; therefore, the more forgiveness he bestows upon anyone, the more he is revered. After a person's return to God, their fear of God is increased for a more honest reason, for they fear God and his goodness, Hosea 3:5, whereas before they feared God and his power, God and his justice. And the Jews, of whom he speaks there, will fear or revere that goodness the more because the sin he has forgiven was so great, as the crucifixion of the Son of God, which, according to their fathers' wishes, rested upon the heads of all their posterity.

God's goodness, once experienced, will make a person afraid to offend him out of sincerity. Self-interest will also make them afraid to provoke that mercy that previously relieved them, to remove them from his favour. When the person was in the deep dungeon, where the chains of sin penetrated their very soul and was bound up under the terrors of the law, when mercy intervened and delivered them and poured oil into their wounds, they will be afraid to provoke that mercy to leave them in the same condition in which they found them, and from where they were drawn. They will be reluctant to be counted among the ranks of transgressors and the bank of galley-slaves from which they were redeemed. They who have tasted the bitterness of sin will fear to commit it, and they who have felt the sweetness of mercy will fear to offend it.

I might add, for others' sake, to encourage them to come to Christ. Every conversion of a great sinner is a new expression of God's love; it is a repeated proclamation of the transcendence of His grace: 'Even when we were dead in sins, hath quickened us together with Christ,' Eph. 2:5, 6. God has given life to those sinful people who were as dark as night and raised them to a state of light. Why? Not just for their own benefit, but so that in the ages to come He might show the surpassing riches of His grace, ver. 7. It was a portrait of God's own heart, exhibited to the world so that they might know, through the gracious treatment and high elevation of those sinners, how generous He is, and will always be, in the distribution of His grace, in order to encourage repentant sinners, as great sinners, to depend on Him in every age. This was His purpose in Paul's conversion in this chapter: 'However, for this reason I obtained mercy, that in me first Jesus Christ might show forth all long-suffering, for a pattern to them which should hereafter believe on Him to life everlasting,' ver. 16; a pattern to them which should hereafter believe on Him. He sets up this apostle as a white flag to invite rebels to treat with Him and return to their loyalty. As every great judgment upon a great sinner is like hanging a man in chains, to deter others from the same practice, so every conversion is not only an act of God's mercy to the convert, but an invitation to the spectators.

This is the argument David uses to persuade God to pour into him the joy of his salvation: 'Then will I teach transgressors Your ways,' &c., Ps. 51:12, 13. I will make all Jerusalem ring with it, and sinners, seeing the multitude and long line of Your tender mercies, will fly into Your arms to be partakers of the same grace. For every great conversion is like a landmark to guide others into a safe harbor. Indeed, he tells God that this will be the outcome of God's pardon to David, Ps. 52:5, 6, which is believed to be written on the same occasion as Ps. 51, when, ver. 5, he had been forgiven, he tells God what the effect on others would be: 'For this shall every one that is godly,' &c., ver. 6, considering it the most appropriate moment to come when God is bestowing His mercy. We see such results when Christ was on earth; when Christ called Matthew, Mark 2:14, the next news we hear, ver. 15, is that many publicans and sinners sat down with Him and followed Him. Many of the same group were encouraged by this kindness to one of their companions to attend to Him.

As when a doctor comes into a house where many are ill and cures one who is in a desperate condition, it encourages the rest to rely on their expertise.

When Christ demonstrates his abilities by converting a sinner close to you, it is a call from heaven not only to excite your emulation to come to him but also to astonish you. For example, the conversion of the Gentiles was intended to provoke the Jews to jealousy: "Salvation is come unto the Gentiles, for to provoke," Rom. 11:11. Indeed, such conversions can more rationally move people to believe than any miracle that objectively stimulates the senses. To see such a remarkable change brought about in the soul of a devil, in a diabolical nature, can be more convincing. If people do not believe in Christ after witnessing such standing miracles, it aggravates their impenitence as much as any miracle that Christ performed on the earth aggravated the Jews' obstinacy. It also puts as black a mark on their character: "And ye, when ye had seen it, repented not afterward, that ye might believe him," Mat. 21:32. Every great sinner that you have seen take heaven by violence is recorded by God as a yet against all your unbelief. Christ can bring hundreds of yet against you on the account of others who have been converted around you. The yet set upon Paul may refer to this, Acts 9:1. In the previous chapter, Luke had described the successful progress of the gospel in Samaria and Jerusalem, which was evidence of the power of this new doctrine, yet Paul proceeded in his persecuting fury against such clear testimonies.

If you had lived in the times of Christ and seen the miracles he performed among the Jews, you would think that you could never have been as foolish as they were and would have immediately believed in him upon seeing those wonders. However, the success of Christ's grace on the souls of men, which you have seen evidence of, is a greater miracle according to Christ himself than the miracles he usually performed, for he tells the apostles that they will do greater works in their conversion work (John 14:12). So your lack of repentance has the same severity as Jewish perversity. Let every conversion of a great sinner be a reason for hope and a spur in your side.

Furthermore, such conversions demonstrate that God's commands are feasible and that his yoke is not oppressive. People naturally believe that God is a harsh master and that his commands are impossible to carry out, but when they see people who had been immersed in sin for many years have a fresh and beautiful growth through grace, and run with delight in God's ways, when they see people who had the strongest prejudices against God's ways thoroughly converted, they may think to themselves, "Why can't I follow those commands? Is it more impossible for me than it was for that person?" It is natural for people not to believe unless they see miracles, "Unless you people see signs and wonders, you simply will not believe" (John 4:48). Therefore, all the ongoing miracles that God has left in the world are the exceptional conversions of men and the worst of men so that people can be convinced of the power of the gospel and the strength of his grace by seeing the impressive results of it on others, as conversion often begins with admiration.

The purpose of this topic is:

1. Firstly, to instruct. The doctrine reveals the power of the gospel. There is nothing that demonstrates the heavenly authority of the Christian religion and the divine effectiveness of the word more than the sudden conversions of notorious sinners. A man entering a church as a tiger and leaving as a lamb. This

small stone is instrumental in laying lusts that are more giant-like than Goliath, down in the dust. When you witness such effects, take them as credentials from heaven, to maintain the credibility of the word, and to assert the authority of that conclusion Paul puts forward, that it is "the power of God for salvation," Rom. 1:16. God gains a reputation for the gospel and the power of Christianity, that can change people from beasts to men, from serpents to saints in a moment.

2. Secondly, to dispel groundless despair. Do not despair of others when you reflect on your own crimes and consider that God never dealt with a baser heart in the world than yours. Wasn't Paul as unlikely to become a convert as any of your relatives who wallow in their blood? Who would have thought that Onesimus would run from his master and be caught in Christ's arms? Nor should you despair of yourself. Should a soul in anguish, covered with penitential blushes, consider itself cast out of the riches of God's affectionate grace? Should any man blaspheme the merciful heart of Jesus Christ so much as to seek relief from a knife, a halter, or a deep well? Even if you were in hell, David tells you that God is with you, even there in His essential presence, even if you were hell itself. For where the devil dwells, that is hell, yet if the soul throbs, sighs, and groans under it, His infinite grace will break down the door and come in upon you. And we know that neither she who had seven demons nor he who had a legion was strong enough to keep out Christ.

Secondly, Comfort of this subject. If God has made you, a great sinner, the object of his mercy, you may be assured of:

1. Continuation of his love. He pardoned you when you were an enemy, will he leave you now that you are his friend? He loved you when you had erased his image and picture to a great extent from your soul, will he hate you now that he has restored that image and drawn it with fresh colours? He justified you when you were ungodly, and will he cast you off since he has been at such pains for you and written in you a counterpart of his own divine nature in the work of grace? Were his compassions first moved when you had no grace, and will they not sound louder since you have grace? Would a father embrace his son when his garments smelled of swine, and cast him off after he has put on him a royal robe? Will Pharaoh's daughter pity Moses when he is in the ark and scorn him when he is dressed?

2. Supplies of his grace. You had a rich present of his grace sent to you when you could not pray for it, and will he not much more give you whatever is needful when you call upon him? He found you when you did not seek him, and will he hide himself from you when you are inquiring after him? A wise

builder does not begin a work when he is not able to finish it. God considered, before he began with you, what charge you would stand him in, both of merit in Christ and grace in you; so the grace he has given you is not only a mercy to you, but an obligation on himself, since his credit is engaged to complete it. You have more unanswerable arguments to plead before him than you had, namely his Son, his truth, his promise, his grace, his name, wherein you had not the least interest. To what purpose has God called and marked you if he does not intend to supply you with as much grace as shall bring you to glory? To what purpose should a creditor forgive part of a debt and lay the debtor in prison for the other part? Has God given you Christ, and will he detain anything else? Supplies of wants, grants of anything you desire, are but as a few grains of pepper that the grocer puts in as an overplus to many pounds.

3. Strength against corruptions. Can small obstacles stand against him who has levelled mountains? Can a few clouds withstand the melting force of the sun, which has dissolved those black mists that covered the sky? Similarly, the remains of your corruption cannot stand up against his power, which has thrown down the great hills of the sins of your natural condition and has dissolved the thick fogs of your unregeneracy. You cannot doubt his strength or his love; love delights in doing the greatest things, and he has already done the greatest, so will he not also do the least? When Moses killed the Egyptian, it is said that he 'supposed his brethren would have understood that God intended by his hand to deliver them,' Acts 7:25. Moses was a type of Christ: if Christ overthrew a whole army of Egyptians that not only pursued you but also kept you in slavery, and he overturned them all in the Red Sea, would you not take notice that he intends to be your deliverer from the scattered troops of them?

Thirdly, Exhortation. 1. To those that God has dealt with in this way.

1. Praise God for his grace. Admiration is all the glory you can give to God for his grace, seeing you can add nothing to his essential glory. Christ will come at the last day to be admired; I pray send your admirations beforehand to attend him at his coming. Who made you thus to differ from another? Was it not God? Let him, then, have the glory. If he made you to differ from others in the enjoyment of his mercy, you should also differ from others in the sounding of his praise. If you have an angel's state, it is fitting you should have an angel's note. If David, when he considered the glorious heavens God had made for man, cried out so affectionately, 'What is man, that you are mindful of him!' Ps. 8:4; surely when you consider that work of grace which God has wrought in you, you may with astonishment cry out, Oh, what is man that you are mindful

of him! What is such a vile creature, that you should take him into your bosom? For there is not a grace in you but is more glorious than the sun with all its regiments of stars, and is more like to God than the great fountain of light with all its amazing splendour. It is something of that heaven which is more glorious than all the rest of the heavens, and is above the reach of the natural eye. Oh what is man, that you are thus mindful of him, to make him, who is a hell by sin, to become heaven by grace! Pardon of but one act of sin makes us forever debtors to God; because one sin renders us obnoxious to eternal torments, and every sin includes a hatred of God. What, then, is it to remit such vast sums, if to pardon one be a miracle? To pardon many committed against a suffering Christ who has invited us, and repeats his invitations, after they have been rejected, is a miracle of the greatest magnitude, something above a miracle!

How should you think Jacob's expression in temporal mercies, a few sheep, too mean, 'I am less than the least of all thy mercies,' Gen. 32:10. Oh I am less, less, less than the least of all this mercy. A great sinner, when converted, should sing a note somewhat above David's 'What shall I render?' Ps. 116:12; and should say, I can render nothing, nothing; but I will render praise, blessing, amazement, astonishment; that is all I can render, and I cannot render enough of that. Had you chosen God first, it would have been some ingenuity in God to answer that affection; but God chose you first, and that when there was nothing lovely in you, when he saw you the most deformed creatures in the world. There was no likeness between God and thee. "Similis simile amat" is a rule in nature, but in this case, "Deus optimus diligit hominem pessimum."

It is that which does amaze the disciples; they could not tell the reason why Christ should manifest himself to them, John 14:22. Perhaps you are only snatched out of a family; the wrath of God may have fallen upon the rest, and you only escaped. Has he not lopped down many cedars in morality and chosen you, a thorn, a shrub, to deck heaven with? Are not many damned that were not guilty of your sins?

How wonderful is it that such a black firebrand should be made a statue fit for glory! He might have written your name as easily in his black book as in his white. Is it not admirable mercy for a God provoked, to take pains with stiff-necked sinners, and to beat down mountains of high imaginations, to rear up a temple to himself? If mercy had knocked once or twice, and no more, you would have dropped into hell; but mercy would not leave knocking. Perhaps your sins were so great that if you had gone but a little farther, you would have been irrecoverable, but God put a stop to the proud waves, saying, 'Hitherto shall you go, and no further.'

2. Often recall to mind your former sin. It was the custom of the saints of God in the past. When Matthew lists the twelve apostles in Matthew 10:3, of whom he was one, he remembers his former profession, "Matthew the tax collector," but none of the other evangelists call him that in that list.

(1.) It makes us more humble. Thoughts of pride cannot stay with us when we frequently remember our rags, chains, and shackles. What was there in your former life but misery to move God to show mercy to you? Although Paul had a greater revelation than any we read of, indeed, than Christ himself had (for we do not read that Christ was caught up into the third heaven), how often does he recall his sin of persecuting to maintain his humility and halt the growth of pride.

(2.) It will make us thankful. A sense of misery increases our obligation to mercy. Those at sea are most grateful for deliverance when they contemplate the danger of the preceding storm. A long night makes a clear morning more welcome.

(3.) It will make you more active in the practice of that grace which is opposed to your former sin. Christ asked Peter three times whether he loved him in John 21, to silently remind him of his recent sin and to have a threefold expression of his love, proportionate to his threefold denial.

(4.) It will be a protection against falling into the same sin again. Perhaps Christ might urge Peter's love with that threefold demand, to renew his repentance for his apostasy, as the best remedy against falling into the same sin again. Therefore, Peter was upset when Jesus asked him the third time, not so much because of his Master's suspicion of his faithfulness, but because of the justified reason for his concern about Peter's fall. And at this third question, Peter remembered his denial and renewed his grief for his previous unworthy behavior. So, look back on your former sin, but with anger and shame, to strengthen your detestation, to suppress your former enjoyment of it, and to magnify the mercy of God, who has delivered you from it. When the Corinthians were proud of their spiritual gifts, the apostle humbled them by reminding them of their cursed state: "You know that you were Gentiles, carried away to these mute idols," 1 Cor. 12:2. When a convert frequently reflects on what they once were in their unregenerate state, they would not return to that state again for all the honours, profits, and pleasures of the world, such great pleasure they take in the work of the new creation.

The second part of the exhortation is for those who are in a state of doubt. The main objection they make is the greatness of sin. "Oh, there was never such a great sinner in the world as I am! If you search all of hell, you will not find another like me. Surely God will never forgive me; my sins are too great to be forgiven." Such language is sometimes spoken by men, partly urged on by the devil to disparage that royal prince Jesus, who came to destroy his works and to keep up enmity between God and man, making the creature have jealous thoughts of the Creator. And partly from a person's conscience, which, acting by those legal principles written in the heart by nature, which are directive and condemning upon non-observance, but discover nothing of pardoning grace. This was the first act of natural conscience in Adam after he sinned; he had the least thought of forgiveness, for he thought only of how he might escape from the presence of God. If you persist in such speeches, they discredit your Creator and argue that you are one of Cain's descendants, who indeed told God to his face that his "sin was greater than could be forgiven," Gen. 4:13. I will argue a little with those who think this way.

But, first, are you really the greatest sinner? I can hardly believe it. Have you ever sinned at the rate Paul did? Or were you ever possessed by such fury? Surely there have been some sinners as great as you are, even if you are as bad as can be. If you were to look over the names of all those in heaven and ask them what sins they were guilty of before God showed mercy to them, I cannot think that you wouldn't find many that would match you, and even exceed you too. You cannot charge yourself with any black circumstances, but you would find someone who would say, "Oh, I was in the same condition, and even worse!" What do you think of Christ's murderers who resisted the eloquence of his sermons and the power of his miracles? And when his death had darkened the sun, shook the earth, and split the rocks, and rent the veil of the temple in two, not one heart among that murderous crew had any saving relentings that we read of. And yet, some of these were converted by Peter's sermon, and the pardon of them left on record by the Spirit of God.

Haven't some of God's greatest favourites been the greatest sinners? Didn't Adam bring the guilt of all his posterity upon himself, and in some sense be charged with the sins of all those who came out of his loins, even all mankind? Yet, the first promise of the gospel was made to him, even before any sentence was pronounced against him for his sin, Gen. 3:15.

Secondly, even if you are the greatest sinner, is staying away from Christ the way to make all your sins less? Are you so rich as to pay this great debt out of your own revenue? Or do you have any hope in another surety? Did anyone, man or angel, tell you they could satisfy for you? Can complaints of a great load, without endeavoring its removal, ease the back that bears it?

Thirdly, Are your sins the greatest? Is not avoiding Christ making them greater? Doesn't God command you to come to Christ? And isn't your delay a greater act of disobedience than your humility can be a complaint of your sinfulness? Don't you have enough burden already? But do you want to add unbelief, which is as bad as all your other sins combined? Isn't a refusal of his mercy provoking? You are crazy if you think that your sin can decrease by trampling upon Christ's heart and rejecting his compassion. You have sinned against justice, against wisdom, against common providence. Isn't this enough, but you also want to rob him of an opportunity to show the riches of his grace, by refusing the blood of his Son, which his wisdom devised and his love offers? Who is persuading you to stay away from Christ? Is it God? Show me where he says so? Show me your authority from God's warrant. But since you cannot, I am sure it is your own corrupt heart and the devil in league together. And can't you say of him far better than Ahab did of Micaiah, 'You never prophesied good to me'? No, he never did, nor ever will. What, do you want to make yourself even worse by following the devil's advice instead of obeying God's command? If your sin is great, let it multiply your tears, but do not let it stop your progress to Christ.

Fourthly, If your sins were less than they are, you might not believe in Christ so easily, as you can now. If you will not believe while your sins are great and your heart is wicked, I can assure you, if your heart were not wicked and your sins little, you still would not believe, because you would be inclined to believe in your own heart and trust in your own righteousness, rather than believe in Christ. Great sins and a wicked heart felt and lamented, are rather an advantage, like hunger is an incentive for a man to seek food. If people had clean hearts, they would probably use them differently and think Christ should come to them. People's poverty should make them more importunate rather than more modest. To say, "I will not come to Christ because I have great sins," is like saying, "I will never have anything to do with happiness if it is offered, because I have great misery. I will not go to a surgeon because my wound is so great. I will not eat bread because I am so exceedingly hungry and likely to starve." This is bad logic, and so it is with you to argue that because you are unclean, you will not go to the fountain to be washed, or to think to be sanctified before believing. Now since you have, as you confess, no righteousness to trust in, I think you should be more easily persuaded to throw yourself upon Christ, since there is no other way.

If, therefore, you are afraid of drowning under these mighty floods which roll upon you, I think you should do as men ready to perish in the waters, catch hold of that which is next to them, though it be the dearest friend they have; and there is none nearer to you than Christ, nor any such friend; catch hold, therefore, of him.

The greatness of your sin is a ground for a plea. Turn your sins into arguments, as David does, 'for it is great,' Ps. 25:11; some translate it, 'though it be great;' and the Hebrew word כי will bear both. The psalmist uses two arguments, God's name, and the greatness of his sin. And both are as good arguments as they were then. You may go to God with this language in your mouth; Lord, my impurity is great, there is more need, therefore, of your washing me; my wound is deep, the greater is the necessity of some plaster for a cure. What charitable person in the world would not hasten a medicine, rather than refuse to grant it! What earthly physician would object, The disease is great, therefore there is no necessity of a cure; therefore there is no room left for my skill! And shall God be less charitable than man? Dogs may lay claim to crumbs that fall from the master's table. You may also use the argument of God's name. Sinners may plead for grace upon the account of God's glory, viz., the glory God will have by it. His wisdom is eminent in serving his own ends by his greatest enemy. His power in conquering sin, his grace in pardoning. Show him his own name, Exod. 34, and see if he will deny any letter of it.

If your illness were not so serious, Christ's glory would not be so impressive. The forgiveness of such sins emphasizes the mercy and skill of your Saviour. The number of demons that were in Mary Magdalene are documented to demonstrate the power of the Saviour who expelled them and accomplished such a significant transformation. Are your sins the greatest? God, who loves to showcase His free grace in the most outstanding manner, will be pleased to have such a great sinner follow the chariot of it, and thus reveal its irresistible power. Use David's reasoning in Psalms 37:12, where in verse 8, he prayed that God would free him from his transgressions, and in verse 12, he used this argument, that he was a stranger. I know no reason why this may not apply to you, for if your sins are significant, you are further estranged from God than the average person. Lord, you command us to show kindness to strangers, to love our enemies; and will you not extend the same mercy to a stranger that you command others to use, and show the same love to such a great adversary as I am? The more significant my hostility, the more magnificent will be your love.

Therefore, plead 1, the infinity of God's mercy. It is strange if your debts are so immense that the treasury of the King of Kings cannot pay them off. Why should the apostle say that God was "rich in mercy" in Ephesians 4 and call it "great love" if it were only expended on minor sins and if any debts could exhaust it? Surely, an infinite God cannot be merely rich in a finite manner. If God is rich in mercy, He is undoubtedly infinitely rich. You cannot assume that those who made it to heaven before you have depleted His riches, for then it would be finite, not infinite. They were not unsearchable riches if the sins of the whole world could exhaust them.

God regards his grace as the most significant part of his wealth. He calls it his riches, which is a title he does not bestow on any other attribute. Riches are not meant to be hoarded and wasted, but to be invested and traded with, and the more they are traded with, the more wealth they generate. God does not delight in keeping these riches to himself, and hoarding them for no use, for "omne bonum est sui diffusivum," which means that the more goodness anything possesses, the more it spreads itself. God loves to distribute his wealth on his own terms, and to risk grace's riches so that he can have returns of glory's riches. Therefore, if you come to God, you have access to all his wealth. Until you can be as sinful as God is merciful, or as evil as God is good, do not think that your iniquities can stop an all-powerful goodness. Mercy holds the greatest influence in God's name, as shown in Exod. 34:6-7. There is only one letter of his power, two of his justice, and nine or ten expressions of his mercy. His power accompanies his mercy and his justice, so on mercy's side against justice, there is a ratio of five to one, which is great odds.

Therefore, plead with God, "Lord, it is said in your word, 'Say not to your neighbour, Go, and come again, and to-morrow I will give you when it is in the power of your hand to do it,'" (Prov. 3:28). Should a man not be willing to give to his neighbour when he has it with him? And shall the merciful God deny me the mercy that I beg for on my knees when he has it all in store for him? Must I forgive my brother if he offends seventy-seven times, a double perfect number? And must I be more charitable to man than infinite mercy will be to me? Will your justice only speak and your mercy be silent, and not plead anything on my behalf? Haven't you said that you are the one "who blots out transgressions for your own sake?" (Isa. 43:25) and that you "blot out iniquities like a thick cloud?" (Isa. 44:22). Is there any cloud thick enough to overpower the melting power of the sun? And will a cloud of sin ever be so thick as to overpower the power of your mercy? Doesn't your mercy have the same strength and eloquence to plead for me as your justice has to argue against me? Is your justice better equipped with reason than your kindness with compassion? Doesn't your compassion have eloquence? Oh, who can resist its pleasing rhetoric!

2. Christ's, and God's intention in his coming, was to forgive great sins. He was called Jesus, a Saviour, because he was meant to save his people from their sins. And do you think that some of his people's sins were not as great as any sins in the world? To save only from minor transgressions would not have been a suitable work for the glorious name of Jesus. We cannot imagine how Christ would have bound himself so strictly to his Father as a surety only for smaller debts. If this had not been his intention, he would have put some limitation in that prayer he taught his disciples, and not have commanded them to pray, 'Forgive us our trespasses,' but forgive us our minor sins or sins of such a size. He never asked what sins, and how many sins, people were guilty of when they came to him; but upon faith, he said, 'Your sins are forgiven.' Plead, therefore, with Christ and say, "You came to do your Father's will, which was that none should be cast off that come unto you, and you have said the same. It is not sufficient for you to say it merely and not do it. Will you draw me with the cords of a man (for I could not come to you unless you draw me), and shall I be beaten back with a frown?"

3. Christ's death was a satisfaction for the greatest sins, both *ex parte facientis*, Christ, and *ex parte acceptantis*, God; for God could not accept any satisfaction but what was infinite. 'One sacrifice for sins for ever,' &c., Heb. 10:12; not one sin, but sins; not minor sins, but sins without exception. Yea, and it is all sin, 1 John 1:7; and all includes great as well as minor. Satan once came to a sick man, and showed him a great catalogue of his sins, concluding from there his eternal damnation. The sick man, strengthening himself by the word of God, bid the devil write over the catalogue in big letters those words, 1 John 1:7, whereupon the devil immediately leaves him.* Can your sins be greater than Christ's merit? or your offenses than his sacrifice? It is strange if the malignancy of your sin should be as infinite as the virtue of his death. He has satisfied for all the saints that ever came to heaven, and put your sins in the balance with theirs, and surely they cannot weigh as much. He was 'a propitiation for the sins of the whole world;' and are your sins as great as the sins of the whole world? If part of his merits is enough to save ten thousand damned souls in hell, if they had applied it, is it not enough to satisfy God for your sins, which are far less? Was not Christ

charged with as great sins as yours can be when he was on the cross? Or are your single sins bigger than all those the prophet means when he says, 'And the Lord has laid on him the iniquity of us all'? Isa. 53:6.

Well, then, plead your Saviour's death, since it was for his honour to satisfy for sins of so deep a dye. It is said in your word, it is a joy to a righteous person to perform judgment, and shall it not be much more a joy to the righteous God? Behold, here I offer you the atonement your Son and my Saviour has made, and if it is not enough, I am content to perish. But if it is, I desire you to do me justice with that joy that a righteous person would do it with, and discharge my transgressions. And if you object that I have flung away this satisfaction and would not have it, I answer, my Saviour's satisfaction was for such sins as those, otherwise none would be saved. For was there anyone who refused the proffer of it at first, made demurs before they entertained it? Let your objections be what they will, Christ shall be my advocate to answer for me.

4. Christ is able to take away great sins. Did he ever let anyone that came to him with a great infirmity go back without a cure and dishonour himself so much, as that it should be said, it was a distemper too great for the power of Jesus to remedy? And why should there be any sin that he cannot pardon? It is as easy for him to heal the one as the other. For he did with as much ease and delight say, 'Your sins are forgiven you,' as say, 'Take up your bed and walk.' Do you have seven devils? Suppose a legion, i.e. six thousand six hundred and sixty-six; he did dispossess a body of as many. Can he not as easily dispossess a soul? If you had ten thousand legions, I dare say Christ would not lose an opportunity of such a conquest. For it would please him more to do great works than little and to show how far his power could reach.

Without such objects, we could not know whether he could 'save to the utmost,' or not, Heb. 7:25. What is his ability for? To be idle? No, it is to be exercised in the most difficult tasks. Suppose the scroll of your sins was as long as it could reach from earth to the highest heavens, would this be beyond the utmost of Christ's ability? Even if you had sinned as much as any person in the world can sin, you are still not beyond the scope of Christ's saving power. I am certain that the word "utmost" can answer all your objections. Even if you had all the sins of the damned in hell upon you, you could not challenge either his free grace or vast power. His blood has the power to make even the devil commence a glorious angel if poured upon him. What is either a great or a light disease to omnipotence when he can cure both the greatest and the least ailments with the same word?

But the soul may ask, I do not doubt his power, but his will. Therefore,

5. **Christ's nature leads him to show mercy to the greatest sinners.** Some people question whether Christ will forgive them because they see him as a harsh master who will not forgive easily. But Christ gives another description of himself, Mat. 11:28, 29, when he urges people to come to him. He tells them that they should not regard him as having a harsh and unforgiving nature but as meek as they are sinful. Meekness is seen in forgiving injuries, not remembering them to breed and nurture revenge. Now, the greater the provocation, the more transcendent is that meekness to let it pass. Did he ever reproach anyone for their offences or throw their former excesses in their face? Luke 7:44. Christ narrates Mary's acts of kindness towards him, but not a word about her foul transgressions. Are your sins so great? Certainly, Christ, who delights in his compassion, will not miss such an opportunity to show both his power and his pity towards such a person. If there cannot be a greater sinner than you, he is unlikely to have such an opportunity again if he misses you.

6. **Christ was exalted by God for this very reason:** 'Therefore he is able to save completely those who come to God through him,' Heb. 7:25. How does Christ become so able to save completely? It is 'because he always lives to intercede for them.' For whom? For those who come to God through him. What is Christ's life in heaven for, if not to intercede? And would his Father's love for him, and the greatness of his interest in God, be revealed by granting some small requests, the forgiveness of a few and minor sins? Christ is consecrated as a priest by God's oath, Heb. 7:28; would God swear for a trivial matter, a thing of little importance? What is the purpose of this oath? Compare it with: 'People swear by someone greater than themselves, and the oath confirms what is said and puts an end to all argument. Because God wanted to make the unchanging nature of his purpose very clear to the heirs of what was promised, he confirmed it with an oath,' Heb. 6:16–18; and the result is that you 'might have great confidence.' What great comfort could there be if only small debts were forgiven? What is the purpose of an oath? Verse 16 says, to put an end to arguments. People do not argue with God, or doubt his mercy in forgiving minor sins, because they think it will be done automatically. But the great struggle that people have with God is about his willingness to forgive great debts, scarlet sins: the struggle is between God and doubting sinners on this account; therefore, to bring this struggle to an end, God has sworn that Christ will be a priest forever, to end all argument between him and believing sinners. For whom is this great confidence based on God's oath? For those who 'have fled to take hold of the hope set be-

fore them,' verse 18. Now, the cities of refuge were not established for ordinary crimes, but for blood, to protect the offender from the avenger.

Shall I add further, God is most pleased with Christ when he makes intercession for the greatest transgressors. Suppose you had been one of Christ's murderers, and had given your vote against him; perhaps you would have thought this a more heinous sin than any you are guilty of. You know Christ prayed for their pardon while he was on the cross; and God gives this as one reason why he would exalt him: 'He shall divide him,' etc., Isa. 53:12. Why? 'Because he poured out his soul to death.' What purpose would there be for him to bear sin, if God had no intention to forgive it? And because 'he was numbered among the transgressors,' which the evangelist understands as his being crucified with thieves, Mark 15:28. Therefore his making intercession for transgressors must be understood as his prayer on the cross. If God exalted him for this, would God be pleased with him, or would Christ fulfil the purpose of his exaltation, if he did not continue to make intercession for sinners of the like kind? Go and tell God that he sent Christ to bless you, Acts 3:26, in converting you, and ask Christ to do his duty.

7. Christ is entrusted by God to distribute his grace to great sinners. Christ is God's Lord-Almoner for the distribution of redemption and the riches of his grace. To whom? Not to the righteous, as they have no need for it, but to sinners, and those who have the greatest need. He would be a poor steward who, when entrusted by his lord to give alms to the poor, overlooks the most miserable, needy, and necessitous individuals when they ask for it and assists those who do not have such pressing needs. Christ is a priest for the same purposes as the legal, typical priests were. They were to have compassion, Heb. 5:2, to measure out their compassion, to offer the sacrifice based on the nature of the sin of the person who presented it. Similarly, Christ, by virtue of his office, is to distribute his grace according to the magnitude of a person's need, as manna was to be gathered according to each person's wants.

To conclude this exhortation, then, have the courage to approach Christ. This is the apostle's purpose in all his preceding teachings, as stated in Heb. 10:19, and so on. God does not demand a heart free from sin, but one that is honest. Who needs more courage than great sinners? And the apostle puts no limits on it. Let us, who have been as great sinners as any, make the same decision as Jeremiah's people in Jer. 3:22. They had both a command and a promise. "Return," was the command. "I will heal," and so on, was the promise. Immediately they responded, "We will come to you," and so on. They seem to have taken the promise out of God's mouth. How will these quick and eager converts stand against your sluggishness and reluctance on judgment day! Shall they do this with only one promise, while you, having all the promises in the book of God repeated to you, give no other answer than "We will not return" or "We dare not come, we dare not believe you"? Did God give Adam only one promise, which he accepted and lived on for his entire life (for we read of no other promise he had than that of the seed of the woman crushing the serpent's head), and yet you will not return when you have so many promises, filling every page in the Scripture?

Have you not many examples? Did not God save all of His saints from the lowest state, with all their rags, and clothe them? Were any of them born princes and sons of heaven? Alas, every person initially asked for a Saviour as a sinner, and all pleaded in the court of heaven as paupers. Were they not in debt, and could they do anything that might make God cross out one of those debts they owed Him? Oh, do not think that you can dam up that flood of love that has flowed so freely to the world for so many ages. Although your illness is severe, it is not irreversible, provided that you go to the physician. He can with a breath burn up your corruption, as quickly as dissolve the creation. Christ can turn the dirtiest water into such wine that can please the heart of God and people. If you have been vessels of sin, and you will be vessels of repentance, God will make you overflowing with mercy. Do not plead your own unworthiness. A person's unworthiness has never stopped the flow of God's kindness. It is too weak a barrier to stop the current of God's favour. The greater your unworthiness, the greater opportunity free grace has to demonstrate its uncontrollable excellence. That person dishonours God who places their sin above God's goodness, or their unworthiness above God's condescension. You cannot do God a greater favour than to come to Him to be made clean. When He enumerates your sin, it is not with a rebuke, but a compassionate sigh, Jer. 13:27. He longs for the time of your return and reminds you of your sin, so that you may seek a remedy sooner, and wonders why you would remain in such a filthy state for so long.

Fourthly, this subject suggests a caution. 1. Do not think your sins are forgiven because they are not as great as those that God has forgiven in others. This is to take comfort in the faults of others. Consider that God rejected Saul for less sins than David committed. Evil angels were rejected for one sin. A few small grains of sand can sink a ship as well as a large rock. Your sins may be forgiven, even if they are as great as others, but then you must have the same qualities as they did. They had great sins, and so do you, but do you have as great a hatred and disgust of sin as they did?

2. Let not this doctrine encourage any person to continue in sin. If you now draw such poison out of this doctrine and boast of the name God proclaims in Exodus 34:6-7, take the cooler with you and remember that it is one part of His name "by no means to clear the guilty." He never intended those mercies for sinners as sinners but as penitents. Penitents, as such, are not guilty, because repentance is a moral revocation of sin and always supposes faith in Christ. There is "forgiveness with God," according to Psalm 130:4, but it is "that He may be feared," not despised. God never intended mercy as a sanctuary to protect sin.

(1.) It is disingenuous to do so. Great love requires great duties, not great sins. The freeness of grace should make us increase in holiness in a more cheerful manner. What high ingratitude it is to be inclined to sin because God is inclined to pardon, to have a frozen heart to Him because He has a melting heart to you! What, to rebel against Him because He has a compassionate heart, and to be wicked because God is good! To turn grace itself into wantonness! Is this to fear His goodness? No, it is to trample on it, to make that which should excite you to holiness a bawd to your lust, and God Himself a pander to the devil. If you thus slight the design of this mercy, which you can never prize at too high a rate, it is certain you never had the least taste of it. If you had, you could not sin so freely, for when grace enters, it makes the soul dead to sin, according to Romans 6:1-2. The apostle answers such a consequence with a "God forbid!"

(2.) It is foolish to do so. Would any person be so naive as to set their house on fire because they have a great river running by their door, from which they may have water to extinguish it, or injure themselves, because there is an excellent plaster that has cured several?

(3.) It is dangerous to do so. If you lose the present time, you are at risk of losing eternity. There are many in hell who never sinned in such a presumptuous manner. God is merciful to the penitent, but he will not be unfaithful to his threats. If you are willing to receive grace, you may have it, but on God's terms. He will not pin it upon your sleeve whether you want it or not. This is to make that which is the aroma of life become the aroma of death to you. See what an answer Paul gives to such a notion, "Let us do evil, that good may come; whose damnation is just," Rom. 3:8. He takes a handful of hell-fire and flings it in their faces. Let Deut. 29:18, 19, stare you in the face, and promise yourself peace in this course if you can: "Lest there should be among you a root that bears gall and wormwood, and it comes to pass, when he hears the words of this curse, that he blesses himself in his heart, saying, I shall have peace, though I walk in the imagination of my heart." As God's goodness is great, which you despise, so the wrath will be the hotter you treasure up. Although great sins are occasions of great grace, yet sin does not necessitate grace. Who can tell whether God would have shown mercy to Paul had he done that against knowledge which he did ignorantly? Repentance must come first; see the order, "Repent, and be converted, that your sins may be blotted out," Acts 3:19. First, repentance and conversion, then justification. This grace is only given to penitent sinners. You do not know whether you will repent, but you may know that if you do not repent, you will be damned. As the gospel binds us to good behaviour as much as the law.